LIBRARY SERVICES FOR ADULT CONTINUING EDUCATION AND INDEPENDENT LEARNING:
A GUIDE

by Raymond K Fisher

with contributions by

Stephen Drodge, Philip Payne and Vernon Smith

*written on behalf of the Library Association's
Sub-Committee on Adult Learning and Libraries*

Library Association Publishing Ltd

1988

Published by
Library Association Publishing Ltd
7 Ridgmount Street
London WC1E 7AE

First published 1988

British Library Cataloguing in Publication Data

Fisher, Raymond K.
    Library services for adult continuing education and
    independent learning : a guide.——(Library Association
    pamphlet : no. 40).
    1. Libraries and adult education——Great Britain
    I. Title   II. Library Association, *Sub-Committee
    on Adult Learning and Libraries*   III. Series
    021.2'4   Z718.8

    ISBN 0-85365-608-8

Photoset in 11/13pt Times by Library Association Publishing Limited
Made and printed in Great Britain by Dotesios Printers Ltd, Bradford-
on-Avon, Wiltshire.

CONTENTS

FOREWORD

In recent years libraries of all kinds have focused on the particular needs of client groups. One of the largest of these target audiences is the adult learner. Arguably it also has the most diverse requirements.

Historically important, because making provision for the adult learner was surely a major objective of the early public library movement, it has perhaps been neglected by the profession (with a few notable exceptions) in favour of more fashionable concerns.

It is greatly to the credit, therefore, of The Library Association that it established a sub-committee specifically to foster this area of library service. One of the many practical outcomes of the work of this committee (now called the Adult Learning and Libraries Sub-Committee) is this guide for librarians in all kinds of library who are providing a service to adult learners. It fills a gap in the literature which any librarian wishing to review the services provided for this important category will find particularly useful as a checklist. Used in this way it will reveal many aspects of service which are capable of improvement, not only for the declared self-learner, but for any purposeful reader. Given current financial restrictions experienced by most librarians, it is noteworthy that many of the suggestions do not require large financial outlays for their implementation. I hope therefore that it will provide a stimulus to librarians to respond to the needs of our users who are taking advantage of the greatly increased range of learning opportunities now available to them. I also hope that the Sub-Committee's ambition that a second edition of this work will be adopted as official Library Association guidelines for this area of service is realized.

If this ambition is to be fulfilled it requires those concerned with provision for adult learners to use this guide and contribute comments, amendments, criticisms and recommendations to the Adult Learning and Libraries Sub-Committee. The first step, however, is for all those interested to read the present work.

Max Broome OBE FLA
President

PREFACE

It is a measure of the Library Association's concern that we have a standing sub-committee devoted to monitoring and developing library support for adult learning. That sub-committee is presently chaired by myself and has on it representatives from different sectors of our own profession, and from the worlds of broadcasting, adult education and educational technology. Our activities have included conferences, responding to discussion documents from all quarters, and receiving reports from our representatives on bodies such as the National Institute of Adult and Continuing Education, the Workers Educational Association, the Open Learning Federation and the Unit for the Development of Adult and Continuing Education.

Library services and librarians are active in many important current support programmes for adult training and learning generally: the Open University, educational information systems and services, Open Tech programmes, learning exchanges of all kinds, independent learning programmes and, most recently, the Open College. It is a difficult area to pin down, both in defining adult learning, and in identifying the particular skills and roles provided by librarians and library services. Adult learning, and library support, are quite ubiquitous and, being so, have often been taken for granted. It is clear that adult learning in all its forms is now high on the agenda of many agencies for its support. It is our hope that these guidelines will not only be of help to our colleagues in libraries, but will serve to explain our roles to the other agencies with whom we often collaborate in supporting adult learning.

The sub-committee is extremely grateful to Raymond Fisher for accepting the task of compiling and editing these guidelines, and to the other contributors. Without his help all this would have remained as committee papers. The work is comprehensive, and the publication is timely. We look forward to seeing these guidelines in use.

John Allred
Chairman,
Library Association Adult Learning
and Libraries Sub-committee

Notes on authors

Raymond Fisher is Librarian, Department of Extramural Studies, University of Birmingham

Stephen Drodge is Head of Department, Curriculum Resources and Information Services, Hinckley College of Further Education

Philip Payne is Planning and Development Librarian, City of London Polytechnic

Vernon Smith is an Educational Consultant and formerly Director of the Scottish Institute of Adult Education

1 INTRODUCTION

1.1 Scope and purpose

1.1.1 The aim of this publication is to focus the attention of librarians on the library and information needs of adult learners and to offer guidelines on how these needs should best be met. Because adult continuing education and independent learning comprise so many activities and processes, both formal and informal, there is often much confusion about which aspects of them are relevant to any particular library, with the result that it is difficult for many librarians to formulate clear-cut policies in this area. It is hoped that the publication of these guidelines will enable librarians more easily to identify those aspects of adult learning which are most relevant in the context of their own library services, and to put into practice those recommendations which are likely to be the most effective. Where the terms 'librarian' or 'library staff' are used in the recommendations they always refer to those professional librarians who have a responsibility either for formulating or for implementing library policy.

1.1.2 Terminology clearly presents a problem: loosely used terms tend to cloud the real issues and hence to make more difficult the formulation of policy. One of the purposes of the present guidelines is to offer precise definitions; these will be given in the appropriate contexts as they arise, but some preliminary definitions are also called for at this stage, as follows: 'Continuing education' may be defined as 'any form of education, whether vocational or general, resumed after an interval following the end of continuous initial education'.[1] It therefore refers to formal, course-based education, whether full-time or part-time, undertaken by any person after the end of their compulsory education. 'Adult continuing education' is therefore any continuing education undertaken by an adult of the age of 21 or over. 'Adult education' is in our context interchangeable with 'adult continuing education'. In other contexts it has often implied the liberal education of adults, while 'continuing education' has been associated with vocational courses. This distinction is not maintained here.

'Independent learning' is any learning activity which does not involve formally enrolling for a course (see also 2.1.1). 'Adult learning' is an umbrella term used here to cover all aspects of adult continuing education and independent learning. An 'adult student' is an adult who has formally enrolled on a continuing education course. An 'adult learner' is in most contexts an umbrella term following the use of 'adult learning'. In others, however, it refers specifically to an 'adult independent learner' and in this sense is quite distinct from an 'adult student'. The context will make this clear. 'Open learning' and 'distance learning' are defined in section 2.2.6.

1.1.3 The scope of the guidelines is the whole of adult learning. They will therefore cover such learning methods and processes as part-time courses, external studies, distance education, open learning, and independent learning. In addition, these aspects will be related to their social contexts, so that reference will also be made, where appropriate, to such questions as domestic and work commitments, leisure, unemployment, training and re-training, retirement and old age, and access to further and higher education. The guidelines will also be concerned with all those institutions and processes which facilitate adult learning, as far as they have bearing on library services, such as educational information and guidance, broadcasting and other media, and inter-institutional co-operation.

1.1.4 For our purpose an adult is any person of the age of 21 or over. The guidelines therefore exclude students in the 16 to 20 age group undertaking formal courses of further or higher education.

1.2 Origin and method
1.2.1 When *Standards for university extra-mural libraries* was published it was stated that they were 'the first part of what is

intended to be a general set of standards for all library services to adult education'.[2] Since then it has been realized that it would be unrealistic to attempt to produce quantitative standards for so large an area of activity, and that general guidelines would prove more helpful. This view has been endorsed by the Library Association's Sub-Committee on Libraries and Continuing Education (now the Adult Learning and Libraries Sub-Committee), which was established in 1979. The first objectives of this Sub-Committee were to monitor developments in the whole field of continuing education and to make librarians more aware of their potential role in it.

Part of the strategy for achieving the latter was the holding of national conferences and regional meetings. It was only after making some headway in this respect that the Sub-Committee turned its attention to the second main part of its terms of reference, which is to 'produce guidelines to advise practising librarians of the ways in which they can adequately meet the needs of existing and potential adult learners'. The need for such a publication was seen in the growing importance of continuing education in society as a whole. After various draft outlines, relating to different types of library, had been produced by different members, it was decided to assign the task of producing the guidelines to one member. At the same time the Public Libraries and Adult Independent Learners project produced its final report,[3] which included a set of guidelines for public libraries. Chapter 4 of the present publication is based on this report; most of the other chapters have been written by the editor, apart from chapters 6 and 7 which are also based on individual contributions.

1.2.2 The present guidelines aim to present a reasonable achievable level of library provision and service, not an abstract statement of ideals. Each chapter is therefore based on the observation of current practice and on the identification of achievements and future potential. In chapter 2 the library needs of adult learners are outlined in general terms; and chapter 3 contains general recommendations which may be applied to all library services. Chapters 4–9 deal with particular types of

3

libraries; each of these chapters ends with a brief summary of recommendations, a short bibliography, and other relevant information. There is intentionally some degree of overlap and repetition between these chapters, so that if necessary librarians may refer to each of them as a largely self-contained unit. The last two chapters consist of a summary of all the main recommendations and a combined bibliography.

1.3 The principles on which the guidelines have been based

1.3.1 The difference between standards and guidelines is that the former offer precise means of *measuring* the adequacy of a service quantitatively, and state what a service *must* do in order to meet certain criteria, while the latter define the questions which should be asked for *evaluating* a service qualitatively and *recommend* certain courses of action towards an effective service. Standards may be the more suitable for a highly specialized, closely defined service, while guidelines are the more suitable for a wide-ranging service which involves a large number of variables.

1.3.2 We are therefore dealing here with questions of choice, policy decisions involving choice between different possible priorities. With greater emphasis in society on continuing education, librarians now have more opportunities for serving the learning needs of the adult community. But in the present economic climate there are strong pressures for *reducing* services, and any guidelines should recognize that some activities or services may have to be discarded if a new policy is to be implemented. We may even have a conflict of values: for the public librarian it may be a conflict between serving the needs of 'the general public' and serving the needs of special groups; for the academic librarian it may be a conflict between serving the needs of the traditional internal, full-time students and those of the non-traditional, external, part-time students. These are not simply economic questions but they are questions which involve the principle of equal access and so touch on the philosophical basis of librarianship.

4

1.3.3   The present guidelines are therefore based on the principle of choice. This principle involves the identification of certain needs, and the encouragement of librarians to make a positive attempt to meet these needs. This process also involves the observation of current practice, and an assessment of what librarians can realistically be expected to do in order to improve the present services. In other words, the guidelines are intended to encourage librarians to think about the needs of adult learners, to make policy decisions to put more resources into services to adult learning. They are also intended to show librarians, once these decisions have been made, how these resources can most effectively be used. Implementation of a part of the guidelines by any one library will not involve a vast increase in funding or staffing; but in many cases it is likely to involve a shift from previously held assumptions, a movement towards the educational role of public libraries and the public role of academic libraries, and towards closer inter-institutional co-operation.

References

1 University Grants Committee, *Report on continuing education*, London, UGC, 1981, 1.
2 Library Association, *Standards for university extra-mural libraries*, London, LA, 1978.
3 Council for Educational Technology, *Public libraries and adult independent learners*, London, CET, 1987.

2 THE LIBRARY NEEDS OF ADULT LEARNERS

2.1 Independent learning

2.1.1 It is known that a large proportion of the adult population in Britain engage in learning activities involving self-instruction or self-education.[1] These activities cover the whole gamut of human experience and are carried out for all sorts of different reasons. Sufficient at this point is the definition of adult independent learners given in the CET Report: 'any members of the public who engage in specific learning activities on a regular or an occasional basis—either as individuals or in groups—without formally enrolling for a course with an education or training agency'.[2]

2.1.2 It is important that a librarian should be able to recognize the main characteristics of an independent learner, in order to be able to identify his or her library needs. The following are the main factors to take into account in this process.

Individual or group learning. A person may be learning entirely on his or her own, or as a member of a group (e.g. a family, a club, a community group venture).

Place of learning. A person may be learning primarily at home, at work, in a library, in hospital, or elsewhere.

Social or domestic situation. A learner may be retired, unemployed, single, or he/she may have particular financial or family problems which have a direct bearing on his/her studies, or he/she may have physical disabilities which hinder his/her learning.

Leisure or necessity factor. The learning activity being undertaken may be described as either a leisure activity (e.g. a hobby, travel) or as a necessity (e.g. house purchase) or a combination of the two.

The subject of study. This may be a traditional subject (e.g. French, local history) or an activity (e.g. creative writing, music,

6

joinery, gardening), or a blend of knowledge or skills (e.g. computing).

The level of study. This may be at any point on a range from basic education or literacy, through elementary or introductory to advanced.

Motivation. The reasons for learning may be complex and may range from simple enjoyment to self-fulfilment or career enhancement.

The media used. A learner may have a preference for a particular medium, e.g. broadcasting, books, films, theatre, records, computers.

Institutional links. A learner may be about to undertake, or have recently completed, a formal course of study at an institution, or he/she may even be currently enrolled on a course. He/she may still be classed as an independent learner, as long as his/her present work does not depend upon formal enrolment. For much of the learning which is undertaken within, or adjacent to, formal continuing education is essentially independent and self-directed.

Previous learning experience and level of education. This may range from the most basic achievements (e.g. the ability to speak and to count), with the learner unable or unwilling to use a library, to an advanced level. An example of the former is self-taught or 'instinctive' learning (e.g. child rearing); an example of the latter is independent research (e.g. a local historian).

2.1.3 The library needs of independent learners may be grouped under three main headings: needs for information, needs for materials and facilities, and needs for guidance and support. No learners can be completely independent in the sense of being self-sufficient, and most will recognize that they need assistance.

2.1.4 Information needs include information about

- books and periodicals
- self-instructional materials and 'open learning' packages
- audio-visual and multi-media materials
- radio and television programmes and linked learning materials

- local societies and other organizations able and willing to help learners
- local people willing to help indepdent learners
- services for learners in special client groups (e.g. the handicapped, the housebound)
- other available education and training opportunities for adults.

In providing any of this information a librarian should take into account the relevant factors listed in 2.1.2 in order to give appropriate information.

2.1.5 Needs for materials and facilities include access to

- books and periodicals
- reference materials
- self-instructional materials and packages
- audio-visual materials
- computer software
- recorded radio and television broadcasts
- audio-visual equipment
- photocopying facilities
- typing or word-processing facilities
- study space
- meeting facilities.

In a library context the provision of information about materials rarely stands alone and usually also implies providing access to those materials and to the facilities for making use of them. Once again the factors listed in 2.1.2 should be borne in mind, in order to provide those materials and facilities which are most appropriate to the client.

2.1.6 Needs for guidance and support within a library context include

- advice about the feasibility of learning goals
- help with planning and learning activities
- instruction in the effective use of library resources and facilities
- help with selecting suitable library materials

- advice on how to make the most effective use of these materials
- help with the development of reading and study skills
- help with keeping records of reading and study undertaken.

Clearly the above needs will vary according to such factors as the degree of independence which any one adult learner wishes to maintain, the complexity of the learning project, and the amount of previous experience.

2.1.7   The ways in which these needs are best met will also vary according to the different kinds of library systems involved, and these will be dealt with in the sections on specific types of library.

2.2   Formal continuing education

2.2.1   This section outlines the library needs of those adult learners who are not independent, in the sense that they have formally enrolled, or intend to enrol, for a course with an education or training agency; and their needs are related specifically to the requirements of their course. First there is a brief description of the ways in which adults learn and of the types of courses which they undertake.

2.2.2   Adult students possess experience, a knowledge of life, and this is often the starting point for new learning. Teachers of adults often relate their teaching to the knowledge and experience which their students have already acquired, knowing that in this way they are likely to engage their interest and intellect. In addition, adults tend to value what they are asked to learn in terms of its relevance to their present circumstances (or at least to the not too distant future), and they are less likely (than children or teenagers) to be looking to the attainment of an objective some years distant. This sense of immediacy can be a source of motivation to the students, and so of satisfaction to the teacher.

Most adult students are highly motivated. The vast majority undertake their courses out of choice. Many are busy people who face competing demands on their time. It follows that, far from being a 'captive audience', most are keen to learn. Potentially, therefore, they are valuable clients of any library service.

2.2.3 At any one time about four million adults are engaged in formal adult education in the UK. The amorphous nature of the world of continuing education is seen in the many different kinds of courses available and the many different kinds of institutions and agencies which provide them.

2.2.4 Local education authorities

LEAs are by far the largest providers of adult education in the UK. They are responsible for the wide range of vocational and non-vocational, advanced and non-advanced, courses offered by polytechnics, colleges of higher education and colleges of further education.

Polytechnics lay greater emphasis on applied studies than do universities; they also have more 'sandwich' courses, more part-time students and more mature student entry, and several have developed modular courses involving mixed mode study. They also engage in a substantial amount of non-degree work, including a wide range of short courses (on which mature students predominate).

Many colleges of higher education have also moved into the area of part-time first degree courses, largely in an attempt to break away from a past concentration on teacher training. Some resemble the smaller polytechnics; others, with a substantial proportion of non-advanced work, are more like colleges of further education. Many, in conjunction with the latter, offer 'Access' courses, which have been designed specifically to encourage adults to return to study and which provide a preparation for courses in higher education without formal prerequisites.[3]

Colleges of further education are concerned mainly with non-advanced, career-orientated studies for the 16−18 year olds; however, many also have large programmes of (mainly non-vocational) adult education classes.

Also within the 'public sector' are adult education and community centres or institutes, offering their own (largely non-vocational) programmes of courses for adults, and community colleges (only in certain areas), which usually combine the function of secondary school, youth service and adult education.

Most of the work of the Adult Literacy and Basic Skills Unit also comes under the auspices of LEAs.

Much of the work of the Manpower Services Commission is done through the LEAs. Its Training Division is responsible for promoting and co-ordinating training in industry and for individuals, and its occupational training section operates largely through colleges of further education (in addition to its own Skill Centres).

The main role of the DES' Further Education Unit is to develop the efficient provision of further education in the UK. One of its functions is to undertake curriculum development projects. Many of these projects relate to the Professional, Industrial and Commercial Updating Programme (PICKUP), the aim of which is to stimulate the provision of mid-career vocational courses. Several polytechnics and colleges have made a major commitment to the PICKUP adult training scheme.

There is, therefore, within the LEAs' responsibility, or under their auspices, an almost bewildering variety of kinds and levels of courses coming under our definition of continuing education.

2.2.5 Modes of study also vary widely within LEA provision. Well established are the full-time and sandwich courses and the part-time day or evening courses. More recent experiments include flexible and open learning systems.

2.2.6 An open learning system is one which enables individuals to take part in programmes of study of their own choice, regardless of geographical or social circumstances. There are three main types:[4]

(a) College-based systems, where all the teaching is done in the college or institution, but where the timetable is flexible and students are able to study at their own pace

(b) Local systems, where most of the students live in the college's normal catchment area but study for most of the time at home, with the college providing tutorials, counselling and the normal range of facilities available to other students as well as correspondence teaching; and

(c) Distance systems, in which most of the students are remote from the providing institution and in which the courses provided include packages of learning materials and are very similar to conventional correspondence courses.

The MSC's Open Tech programme, launched in 1982, is a system which promotes the use of open-learning methods in training and updating courses, mainly for technicians and supervisors in industry, and includes features from all three main types. The MSC's Open College, which is a new television and radio training agency, plans to begin transmissions in 1987. It will be used primarily for broadcasting vocational training programmes at sub-degree levels, which will be linked to courses within further and higher education institutions. Courses are expected to lead to qualifications, and particular importance will be attached to the provision of suitable teaching materials to accompany the courses. Finally, many 'Access' courses (see 2.2.4) also contain elements of flexi-study or distance learning.[5] 'Flexistudy' is a form of open learning, consisting of a combination of elements from types (a) and (b). The emphasis is on flexibility of study, i.e. students have a wide range of choice over when and for how long they wish to join a class. Written work schemes are used to structure students' learning, and there is more emphasis on individual tuition than on lectures. Distance learning is also a form of open learning, although again there are differences within it. The essence of it is that students work at home, or at another place of their choice, on centrally produced correspondence courses. Some distance education schemes are highly structured, and allow for little flexibility in the pace or timing of students' work; in others students can be more independent and set the pace of their own work.

2.2.7 The next main category of continuing education provider is that of the long-term and short-term *residential colleges*. The long-term colleges receive DES grant for the provision of the 'liberal education of adults', and offer one-year and two-year courses. The larger number of short-term colleges also offer liberal courses, lasting from a weekend up to three weeks.

2.2.8 *The Workers' Educational Association* has as one of its main objectives 'to stimulate and to satisfy the demand of workers for education'. It works largely through its local branches, which organize classes in which subjects chosen by members are studied in a systematic way. Each of its districts is recognized by the DES as a Responsible Body and receives government grant accordingly. Most of the districts work closely with university extramural departments and organize courses with them through joint committees.

2.2.9 *The universities* are also significant providers of adult continuing education. Several have special schemes for accepting 'mature' students for full-time degree courses. All universities offer part-time courses for adults, including programmes of short post-experience courses (usually organized by the appropriate subject departments) and also liberal adult education courses (mainly off-campus and organized by departments of extramural studies). Most of the large universities are designated as Responsible Bodies and receive DES grant to provide liberal adult education programmes for the general public throughout a clearly defined geographical area. Some offer part-time degree and diploma courses. Unique in the UK is London University's external degree system, through which adults can study independently for the same degrees as those taken by its internal full-time students. London's Birkbeck College specializes in offering part-time degree courses in conventional subjects through evening classes, for adults in employment. A small number of universities have opened some of their regular undergraduate lectures to the general public.

2.2.10 *The Open University* offers opportunities for adults to study at home by distance teaching methods, on general degree courses. Degrees are built up on a credit system, starting with a first year foundation course and going on to other courses at second, third and fourth levels. Teaching is based on printed correspondence materials, set books, and television and radio broadcasts. About 260 study centres, offering face to face teaching and advice, have been established. The Open University also has an expanding programme of non-degree continuing education courses, also using distance teaching materials.

2.2.11 The final category comprises a large number of *other adult education agencies*, including what may be called the 'informal voluntary' sector and the 'private' sector. The voluntary sector includes organizations such as The National Federation of Women's Institutes, The National Union of Townswomen's Guilds, and The Pre-Retirement Association, all of which are engaged in the education of adults. The private sector consists mainly of the correspondence colleges, a notable example of which is the National Extension College. Other organizations which contribute to the provision of learning opportunities for adults include the Armed Services, the Prisons, the TUC and the Unions, the Churches, professional societies and associations, the Adult Schools, the recently established University of the Third Age, and a wide range of firms and 'public bodies' with their own in-house training schemes.

2.2.12 There are some organizations which, while not directly providers of adult education, are closely involved in promoting it. Three examples follow. The National Institute of Adult Continuing Education exists to promote 'the study and the general advancement of adult continuing education'. The Council for Educational Technology promotes the use of new technological developments at all levels of education, as well as in industry and the public services; it is also concerned with the encouragement and documentation of new approaches to the process of learning. The Business and Technician Education Council promotes work-related education and offers nationally recognized qualifications.

2.2.13 The library needs of the many kinds of students coming within this section 2.2 may be grouped under three main headings: educational information and guidance, library education and the acquisition of study skills, and access to library materials and facilities. While these headings are similar to those for independent learners in 2.1 the needs of adult students are seen to be rather different when examined in detail.

2.2.14 Educational information and guidance is one of the primary needs of adults wishing to undertake a formal course of study. All students need to know what courses are available, and many need guidance in choosing what is most suitable for them. Not all students are sure which subjects they want to learn; in addition many face financial, social and educational barriers to learning opportunities and many have particular problems concerning entry qualifications, domestic responsibilities, transport, and the amount of time available for study. The first priority should be to make it as easy as possible for potential students to obtain the basic information which they need, and the second should be to enable them to translate it, if necessary, into terms which they can understand and act upon. It is at this stage that all the factors relating to a student's background and educational needs should be identified, and those listed in 2.1.2 for independent learners are also applicable here. The extent to which librarians should be involved in these processes is discussed in sections 4.6, 5.3, and 5.4.

2.2.15 The acquisition of appropriate study skills and information skills and the ability to use libraries effectively are also important needs which many adult students have before launching into a course of study. For some it may be many years since formal study, while others may have left school at the minimum age and have had little or no post-school education. Many will not have had training in the techniques of learning and remembering, including effective reading, note-taking and essay writing, and in the application of practice from written and diagrammatic explanations (e.g. computing, horticulture). In addition, some may never before have used a library of any kind; certainly many will not know how to make the most effective use of public libraries, and certainly many will be intimidated when first using a large academic library. Again, the extent to which librarians should be involved in the process of meeting these various needs is discussed in sections 4.6.3, 4.6.4, 5.5.

2.2.16 In the need for *access to library materials and facilities* there is clearly some overlap with the needs of independent learners as identified in 2.1.4 and 2.1.5. But here the emphasis will be more on course and institutional, and less on personal, requirements. It follows that more planning should be possible in meeting students' needs. At the same time the keyword for most adult students is immediacy. Many adult students are busy people with job and family commitments and often with long distances to travel to their course meetings. When carrying out a reading or writing assignment they should not have to encounter long delays or complicated bureaucratic procedures before they can obtain the items or the information they require—for otherwise the disadvantages which they may already have are further aggravated. In the case of home based study and distance education the main needs are for delivery of materials from the library to the students and for easy access to bibliographical information.

2.2.17 The main needs for materials and facilities may be listed as follows:

- a course book-list, accurately completed and preferably annotated
- access to books and periodicals
- access to audio-visual and other non-book materials, including recorded broadcasts and computer software
- advice on how to make the most effective use of library materials
- availability of bibliographical aids and other reference materials
- access to computerized literature searches
- access to computerized information services
- access to photocopying facilities
- study space.

The above needs will, of course, vary according to the type and level of subject being studied, the location and length of the course, the teaching methods used, and other factors. In some cases the main objective will be the acquisition of a purely practical skill (e.g. how to tarmac a drive); in other cases the main objective may be purely intellectual (e.g. philosophy).

Clearly the educational goals of a course should be considered when assessing the library needs of any particular student or group of students.

References

1 Brookfield, S., 'Independent adult learning', *Studies in adult education*, **13**, (1), 1981, 15–27.
2 Smith, V., *Public libraries and adult independent learners*, London, CET, 1987.
3 Lucas, S. and Ward, P. (eds.), *A survey of 'access' courses in England*, Lancaster, University of Lancaster School of Education, 1985.
4 Further Education Unit, *The experience of open learning: a summary document*, London, FEU, 1985.
5 Pates, A. and Good, E. (eds.), *Second chance 1984–1985: the annual guide to adult education and training opportunities*, Cambridge, National Extension College, 1984.

Further bibliography

Advisory Council for Adult and Continuing Education, *Distance learning and adult students: a review of recent developments in the public education sector*, Leicester, ACACE, 1983.

Dale, S. and Carty, J., *Finding out about continuing education: sources of information and their use*, Milton Keynes, Open University Press, 1985.

Drodge, S., Libraries and adult learners: future developments, *Journal of librarianship*, **16**, (3), 1984, 170–87.

Jennings, B., *The education of adults in Britain: a study of organization, finance and policy*, Hull, University of Hull Department of Adult and Continuing Education, 1985.

Kennedy, D., *How do I cope? teaching and support in continuing education*, Sheffield, Association for Recurrent Education, 1983.

Library Association, University College & Research Section, *Open learning and its impact on academic libraries*, Nottingham, LA UC&R Section, 1985.

National Institute of Adult Continuing Education, *Yearbook of adult continuing education 1986–87*, Leicester, NIACE, 1986.

Neale, B., *An investigation of the learning needs of adults in Islington*, London, Inner London Education Authority/ London Borough of Islington Library Service, 1983.

Newman, M., *The poor cousin: a study of adult education*, London, Allen & Unwin, 1979.

Open University, *Adults and education* (Unit 14 of Course E222, The control of education in Britain), Milton Keynes, Open University Press, 1979.

Ward, M. L., *Readers and library users: a study of reading habits and public library use*, London, Library Association, 1977.

Tight, M., *Part-time degrees, diplomas and certificates: a guide to part-time higher education courses at universities, polytechnics and colleges*, Cambridge, Hobsons, 1986.

3   GUIDELINES APPLICABLE TO ALL TYPES OF LIBRARY

3.1   Library management involves the setting of aims and objectives. Librarians have to choose the aims of their service from a range of possible needs that could be met. In developing a statement of aims, library staff should carry out a broad survey of the community which they serve. There is a high probability that adult learners (in the broadest sense of the term) will form a proportion of this community.

3.1.1   The above statements apply to special libraries, as well as to public and academic libraries. While chapters 4−8 are devoted specifically to the last two categories, there is no section on special libraries and the present one is to be regarded as the most applicable to them. For special libraries constitute an important information and learning resource. While they must serve primarily the needs of their parent institution, there is a strong case for making their resources available to serious adult students and independent learners, provided that adequate safeguards are established. Therefore, libraries in the commercial and industrial sector, government libraries, the National Health Service, and libraries serving research and professional organizations, should all be regarded as having a potential role in serving adult continuing education.

3.1.2   However, the evidence suggests that adult learning has not yet been given its due weighting in the formulation of policy in nearly all types of libraries. For example, only 23% of the books borrowed from UK public libraries in 1985 were non-fiction,[1] and, in general, academic libraries have been slow to make provision for the growing number of part-time adult students.[2]

3.1.3   In any type of library a choice may have to be made between the competing demands of different groups of users. A librarian should precisely identify the needs of the adult learners within his/her community profile, on the lines of the categories listed in chapter 2, and weigh these needs against those of other groups. In this process the growing importance of adult continuing education in society should be borne in mind. In this way a set of priorities will be established.

3.1.4 Most librarians have to work through an organizational structure; and achieving a possible change in policy, or the allocation of additional resources, will usually involve decisions by a higher committee or by senior management. It is recommended that each chief librarian should have full membership of the appropriate policy-making body, whether it be library committee, local council, academic board, or board of studies.[3]

3.1.5 Librarians who are seeking changes in policy or the reallocation of resources will also need skills in the public presentation of logical arguments. Summaries of such arguments should be circulated to all members of the appropriate committee or board. Such statements should be based on accurate statistical information and should stress that the new (or additional) services required are based on the genuine needs of clients. These needs should be spelled out; and where an existing service has to be curtailed, reasons for this should also be given.

3.1.6 Every library system should thus produce an explicit statement of its aims and priorities, for the benefit of its staff and of its existing and potential users.

3.2 Once the needs of adult learners have been accepted as part of a planned service, resources should be allocated to meet them. The earmarking of resources in this way should be based on as clear an identification as possible of the library needs of adult learners as outlined in chapter 2. A member of the library staff should be designated to be responsible for services to adult learners and for oversight of the use of resources. Wherever such a designation is made, however, measures should be taken to ensure that the rest of the library staff do not leave all the work to the person responsible.

3.2.1 These resources will be used most effectively if there is close co-operation between the library and the relevant educational institutions, information and guidance services, voluntary societies, and other libraries in the region, and a system of co-operation should be established and maintained. The feasibility of establishing regional libraries for adult education in each area should be considered.[4]

3.2.2 In implementing a policy of service to adult learners, particular attention should be paid to those background factors (as described in 2.1.2) which are most prominent in the community profile. Such factors may determine whether the service is to be of the outreach sort, in which the library is an 'agent for change', or of the responsive sort, in which the library offers services which are 'there to be used if desired'.[5]

3.2.2 Particular attention should also be paid to delivery systems, and to solving logistical problems, whether it be delivery of documents, information or advice. For most adults the concept of 'immediacy' is all-important, because of the complexity of their working and domestic lives.

3.3 Once a service has been established, it should be regularly funded, and regularly monitored and measured, in order to maintain its effectiveness. Surveys should be carried out and statistics regularly compiled. The following specific guidelines (in chapters 4−9) should help librarians to measure the effectiveness of the services which they have initiated or which they are developing.

References
1 Publishers Association, *Booktrade yearbook 1986*, London, Publishers Association.
2 Davidson, D. E., 'What will be the bandwagon of the 1980's?, University College and Research Section, *Newsletter*, 1, 1980, 7.
3 See e.g. Ruse, D., 'Academic board membership', *Library Association record*, **89**, (4), 1987, 201.

4   Fisher, R. K., 'Regional libraries for adult education', *Journal of librarianship*, **3**, (4), 1971, 228–36.
5   Allred, J., *The measurement of library services: an appraisal of current problems and possibilities*, Bradford, MCB Publications, 1979, 29.

4 PUBLIC LIBRARIES AND ADULT INDEPENDENT LEARNERS

This chapter consists mainly of an adaptation of the guidelines produced as part of the Council for Educational Technology's project report on Public Libraries and Adult Independent Learners.[1]

4.1 Scope
The general library needs of independent learners, and the main factors to be considered when defining the needs of individual learners, have already been outined in section 2.1. The guidelines in the present section are concerned with the practical development of public library services for such people involved in independent learning activities. Although some libraries may wish to develop special schemes for identifiable groups of adult learners, the majority of arrangements discussed here relate to mainstream library services for the general public.

4.1.2 The public library service has traditionally been concerned with independent learners as well as with 'recreational' readers. However the full extent of independent learning in the community has become apparent only in the last twenty years or so. The decline of the concept of readers' adviser in the 1950s and 1960s perhaps reflected the failure of librarians to recognize their potential in this area. While attitudes are now changing, much remains to be done. Some library authorities have been active in establishing community and educational information services, and in recognizing the importance of staff training in developing a service of assistance to individual learners. But too many library users (and non-users) still have a narrow view of the role of public libraries, which are usually regarded as the place where one goes to get *books* rather than *information* (or other materials or services).[2]

The main needs, therefore, are to raise the awareness of public library staff of the full dimensions of independent learning, and for librarians to publicize more widely the help which they can give to adult learners of all kinds.

4.2 Types of users
Independent learning is not something new or special. The promotion of self-education has long been one of the main purposes of the United Kingdom public library system.

Everyone engages in learning activities, and most librarians are familiar with the following types of users:

- 'Serious readers', who want to tackle subjects or authors in a systematic way
- People engaged in systematic independent study, seeking to extend their general education
- People enrolled in Open Learning courses, but also engaged in private study
- People pursuing their own research projects on an independent basis
- People engaged in self-development or self-directed training, whether employed or unemployed
- People engaged in short-term projects or practical tasks, who need to learn about some particular aspect of their project
- People pursuing hobbies, interests or subjects of personal concern—which might cover anything under the sun
- Members of community groups, clubs and societies which include an educational element within their activities.

4.2.1 It is recommended that each public library service should: (a) review the arrangements for the organization and orientation of library services to meet the needs of independent learners and produce an appropriate development plan, (b) ensure that a senior library manager has overall responsibility for the development of such services.

4.2.2 In producing a development plan, the question of self-help or assisted service needs to be examined first.

The effectiveness of self-help depends on two factors: the deliberate organization of the library to facilitate such use, and

24

the skills and confidence of library users. At the other extreme, the policy of encouraging library staff to do everything for each individual enquirer undermines the motivation of many library users to become independent learners able to do things for themselves.

Each public library service should therefore (a) ensure that the library staff are aware of the needs of independent learners and of the kinds of assistance which the library should be able to provide, and (b) adopt appropriate staff development and training arrangements designed to assist staff improve library services for learners.

4.3 Categories of learner needs

As already stated in sections 2.1.3–7, learner needs, and the related questions on library services, may be grouped under three main headings:

(a) needs for information
(b) needs for materials and facilities
(c) needs for guidance and support.

4.4 Providing information for learners

4.4.1 Most libraries can provide access to a substantial range of *bibliographical information*. However, people do not always make effective use of what is available. In smaller branch libraries up-to-date copies of key reference works may not be available.

− Members of the public should be made aware of the range of bibliographic sources and tools available in the library (and in neighbouring libraries)
− Readers generally should know how to use them effectively
− Staff should offer assistance to users requiring bibliographic information
− Where new technology provides potential access to comprehensive bibliographical data, members of the public should be encouraged to use the equipment concerned−and there should be adequate information (on notices or posters) giving basic instructions.
− Where a library does not have up-to-date copies of key direc-

tories, reference sources, etc., these should be available elsewhere in the community in the hands of individuals or organizations willing to let others have sight of them
− In compiling booklists on particular subjects a distinction should be made between different levels, e.g. beginner, general interest, enthusiast, specialist expert.

4.4.2 Information about *self-instructional or open learning materials* is hard to come by. Whether or not a library service includes these materials in its own stock, it should be able to provide information about them to independent learners.

The library should have staff who are knowledgeable about Open University, Open Tech and other self-instructional materials. The library should provide access to the on-line database of MARIS-NET (Materials and Resources Information Service), which holds information on training materials and resources and an open learning bibliography.

4.4.3 Information about *audio-visual* and *multi-media materials* will be needed by many independent learners. The library service should be able to provide information about a wide range of learning materials.

Arrangements for a new system of bibliographic control for non-book materials are currently under review by the British Library, although home video is unlikely to be included, and separate arrangements are being considered for microsoftware.

In the meantime, the most comprehensive source of information about film and video is the *British national film and video catalogue.*[3]

Information about film and video material available for hire by local groups or individuals may also be obtained from a wide range of agencies (for examples see 4.8).

Users should be informed that the library provides information about audio-visual materials.

Special arrangements should be made for ensuring that organizations seeking audio-visual training materials and community groups seeking audio-visual materials to enrich programme activities are aware of and able to obtain appropriate information.

Liaison or referral arrangements should be made for dealing with enquiries that need to be directed elsewhere.

4.4.4 Information about *broadcasting and broadcast-related materials* should be available.

Many TV and radio programmes offer learning opportunities for adults. As well as learning from a programme itself, viewers and listeners can often send for packs of materials or other publications associated with the programmes.

Each library service should carry adequate information about educative radio and television broadcasting, and associated back-up materials and activities.

Advance information about adult education programming is published in:

(a) *TV take-up* (see 4.8). This gives information about programmes on ITV and Channel 4, and about rules for recording them—and gives details of Community Education Liaison Officers in each TV Company area.
(b) *See 4* (for Channel 4) (see 4.8).
(c) BBC Education Newsletters (see 4.8). These provide information about programmes on both BBC television channels and on BBC network radio.

General information about broadcasting and adult learning in the United Kingdom (including addresses of BBC and Independent local radio stations) will be found in the broadcasting section of the *Yearbook of adult continuing education.*[4]

Information about broadcast-related back-up materials and activities may be obtained: (in England and Wales) from Broadcasting Support Services, (in Northern Ireland) from Educational Guidance Service for Adults, (in Scotland) from NETWORK Scotland Ltd, (for details of these see 4.8).

– Users should be informed that the library carries information about broadcast programmes and broadcast-linked materials
– Both staff and users should be aware that relevant information is broadcast on the various teletext services
– Good channels of communication should be established with appropriate broadcasting agencies and their liaison staff.

4.4.5 Information about *local organizations* is commonly included within a library's wider range of Community Information—and in several places this information is now computerized. However, basic information requested from organizations may need to be supplemented, if the library is to have answers to some of the questions about local organizations which might be asked by independent learners, e.g.

- Does the organization cater for novices and/or for more experienced learners?
- Are the organization's resources, facilities, or equipment made available for general use, or is use restricted to members?
- Does the organization have specialist experts who are willing to offer help and advice to non-members and/or speak to other groups?

- The library should have an efficient system for collecting, organizing, and updating information about local organizations.
- Users should be encouraged to become familiar with, and make use, of the library's Community Information service.

4.4.6 Information about *local people* willing to make their expertise available to others can be used by both secretaries of local groups seeking to diversify annual programmes, and by other people who are looking for tutorial help or advice from a subject specialist.

- The library should provide information about people offering help with various subjects or activities
- Other local agencies should be identified who might be interested in helping the library set up or maintain databanks of relevant information about offers and requests.

4.4.7 Information about *education and training opportunities*
Independent learning and participation in conventional education or training programmes are complementary activities for many people, and many enquirers may need information about a variety of options before deciding which activities to pursue independ-

ently and which via enrolment on a course. Most public libraries carry at least some information about adult, community, further and higher education, adult training, distance education and open learning.

Some public libraries are also already participating, or planning to participate, in the development of Educational Guidance Services for Adults.[5] The potential role of public libraries in educational guidance is discussed in section 5.4 and a definition of guidance is given.

Many public libraries have made a point of collating information for disadvantaged and other special client groups. Two points are important here: (i) to make sure that information about learning opportunities (independent or otherwise) is included, and (ii) to be aware that information and services for a specific client group may also have relevance to a wider range of library users.

- The library should have a system for obtaining and disseminating comprehensive information about education and training opportunities for adults, in particular in association with the rapidly developing systems of ECCTIS, the PICKUP Short Course Directory, and TAP, (see 5.3), and of MARIS-NET (see 4.4.2)
- If there are plans for the setting-up or development of a local educational guidance network for adults, the library should decide what role it will play in organizing or servicing the network
- Library staff should make sure that informal and independent learning (and the services of public libraries) are adequately promoted by those involved in the provision of educational information and guidance services, and by those responsible for training the staff involved
- Library staff should consider what contribution their service can make to the training of educational guidance workers
- Library staff should be aware of the learning opportunities provided for older people, the unemployed, the handicapped and other special client groups.

4.5 Providing materials and facilities

Public libraries may assist independent learners by providing materials on the premises, by lending, by locating collections of materials in suitable community contexts, or by selling materials to the public.

4.5.1 Printed materials

The provision of books, periodicals and other printed materials is a primary function. In theory the local public library offers access—via local, regional and national inter-lending systems—to almost any item of published print material. In practice few library users exploit the full potential of the library system.

Some of the most common problems of less-experienced library users are: ignorance of the fact that the books they see on the shelves are not the only books available; reluctance to use the request system because they are unsure how it works or because books take too long to obtain; and ignorance of the range of suitable books, periodicals, etc., dealing with the subject about which they wish to learn.

- The library should provide clear and attractive information (via leaflets, posters and other suitable means) emphasizing the full extent of its stock and the range of books, periodicals, etc., available via the interlending system
- The waiting time for items requested from other libraries should be kept to a minimum
- The library should offer a service of compiling booklists on request, and (if required) for obtaining such books at the time when they are needed. This service should be publicized
- The library should have systematic arrangements for the promotion and display of books on a wide variety of subjects, aiming to stimulate new interests and to draw attention to books which might not otherwise be noticed by casual browsers

4.5.2 The provision of self-instructional materials and open learning packages

The increase in supply of print and mixed-media packages specifically designed for self-instruction, and the growing numbers of people familiar with home study and self-development programmes promoted under the auspices of the Open University, the Open Tech and other organizations, seem likely to stimulate an increase in demand for such materials via the public library service.

In addition the rapid spread of open learning approaches in the field of adult training and the growing interest in the notion of 'self-development' (in the public service as well as in the commercial and industrial sectors) suggest a possible new role for public libraries as resource banks of training material.

In the education sector, schools, adult, further and higher education institutions (and their libraries) are also beginning to consider arrangements for acquisition and deployment of open learning materials. Sources of information about such materials are given in sections 4.8 and 4.9.

- The library should have special arrangements for obtaining stocks of appropriate open learning materials
- Arrangements should be made for the specialized holdings of such materials on a regional basis, to ensure comprehensive coverage
- If the Education Service (or nearby college or polytechnic) is involved in running or planning an Open Learning scheme the public library should collaborate with it over the acquisition or deployment of open learning materials and over the provision of support services for learners.

4.5.3 Audio-visual and non-book materials

From the point of view of the public, availability of audio-visual and non-book materials (including video and software) is extremely patchy, since every library service makes its own decisions about whether or not to stock any particular type of material, and whether provision is to be made on a free or paying basis.

The problems of availability associated with copyright restrictions remain to be resolved by new legislation. However, the supply of such materials for independent learning could become increasingly important. The rapid progress of interactive video as an aid to independent learning probably means that libraries should also be giving some thought to this medium. The National Interactive Video Centre (see 4.8) can provide information and advice.

One general source of information about audio-visual materials available is the annotated *Distributors' index 1986.*[6] Emphasis is on educational material at post-school level. It lists over 470 distributors in 97 subject categories. The Audio-Visual Groups of the Library Association and Aslib and the joint LA/ASLIB periodical, *Audiovisual librarian*, are recommended as further sources of advice and information.

- The library should provide a service for members of the public wishing to use video material or computer software for learning activities
- The library should participate in an interlending system (and/or a referral system) for audiovisual materials
- The library service should provide viewdata or other videotex services (which might be useful for independent learners).

4.5.4 Broadcast recordings and broadcast-linked materials

Radio and television output represents a rich seam of learning material which might usefully be available (on tape) for the benefit of independent and other learners. It is hoped that some of the present copyright restrictions on off-air recording and programme availability will soon be removed by new legislation, to enable public libraries to provide greater access to recorded programmes. Details of the present rules governing recording of programmes are obtainable from the publications listed in 4.4.4.

- The library should provide access to tapes of radio and television programmes for independent learners
- The library should have information about other agencies in the area which carry tapes of (or which have arrangements for off-air recording of) broadcast programmes, and which would allow use of their tapes by independent learners on a 'reference' basis
- The library should carry stocks of broadcast-linked print material

- The library should locate such materials in the same place as the recorded programmes.

4.5.5 Audio-visual equipment and hardware

The range of audio-visual equipment and hardware available for public use on library premises will reflect, to a large extent, the range of materials and the various media stocked by the library concerned. Libraries providing public access to microcomputers can and do play a significant role in promoting 'Computer literacy'. Word-processing and/or typewriting facilities may be provided in some libraries. Photocopying facilities are almost, and should be, universal.

Clearly only a minority of libraries will be able to provide a full range of equipment; but it would be helpful if information about other service points and other nearby agencies offering access to equipment and media of various kinds were available in libraries. (For reference to Interactive Video see section 4.4.3).

- The library should encourage members to make use of audio-visual equipment and new technology hardware, and this encouragement should be included in library publicity.
- The library should be able to provide direct help, if individuals or community groups need use of audio-visual equipment, or refer them to an agency which can make available the equipment they require.

4.5.6 Study and meeting facilities

It is normal for at least some study space to be provided in all but the very smallest of libraries.

Use of library facilities by community groups will depend on the extent of accommodation available and on arrangements for after-hours opening. Wherever practicable libraries should adopt a policy of maximizing community use, particularly by groups whose members and activities are likely to benefit from use of library resources and facilities (beyond the mere use of library space). Library premises may, of course, also be used for the library's own lecture programmes or other extension activities.

- The library should publicize the fact that study space is avail-

able in the library for use by all members of the public
- If the library has inadequate study facilities, or is not open at times when people need to make use of facilities, arrangements should be made for independent learners to make use of library facilities in a nearby educational institution (or other organization with available study and library facilities)
- The library should have a systematic policy of promoting use of its facilities and services by community groups.

4.6 Providing guidance and support
Many adults will need help with (a) planning their learning, (b) selecting materials (and in general using the library effectively), (c) reading and study skills, and some may need help from subject specialists.

4.6.1 Help with planning learning activities
The process of planning learning goals may depend on finding out exactly what range of services and materials can be made available via the public library system. Consultation with a trained member of library staff can, on the one hand, provide information, help and encouragement for those who have underestimated what might in fact be possible and, on the other hand, help to identify unrealistic ambitions which are likely to lead to disillusion.

Library staff should be trained to deal with such consultations. Staff who are expected to provide effective help for users engaged in independent learning activities will need to be able to:

- detect learning aspirations in an initial enquiry—about a book, or subject or library service
- engage enquirers (briefly) in dialogue, to clarify the nature of the planned learning activity
- encourage and assist users to develop the skills of efficient self-help library use.

Library staff should give positive help in planning reading/learning activities to those members of the public who request it. The library should publicize its system of guidance and assistance for independent learners.

4.6.2 Help with selecting materials

The kind and level of help needed will vary according to the knowledge and experience of the learners concerned. Some users will be self-sufficient; others will need a great deal of guidance. The main danger is that library staff might do all the work on behalf of users, rather than help users to operate the system for themselves.

- The library staff should have adequate knowledge of stock to give useful advice on selection of appropriate materials for independent learners
- The library staff should have a systematic approach which encourages users to learn how to exploit library resources for themselves, rather than to rely on staff to do and find everything for them
- The library service should produce suitably graded booklists or learner guides on a range of selected topics. The availability of such guides should be publicized.

4.6.3 User education

Public libraries should recognize that they have a special responsibility for 'user education' and for the promotion of library and information literacy in the community at large. The user-oriented or market-oriented library will regularly remind its public of the wide range of materials and services which it offers, provide further information about them, encourage regular users and members to try out facilities or services not previously used, and offer special opportunities and incentives for doing so.

There are various ways of training people to use libraries more effectively, and public libraries should be willing to experiment with a range of them. They include: library guides, and other printed information; posters, display notices, instructions, slogans, signs, and guiding; viewdata sequences; microsoftware self-instructional programs; self-instructional video (or other audio-visual programmes); guided tours; open days, special sessions, and practical workshops; illustrated talks; short courses on library and information skills; and the provision of individual help.

- The library service should develop a policy for the promotion of user education and information literacy
- The library should have a member of staff with special responsibility for promoting user education
- The library's policy of helping and encouraging the development of library and information skills should be publicized to users
- Opportunities should be created for promoting library and information literacy in community contexts outside the library itself.

4.6.4 Help with reading and study skills

Libraries should be as much concerned with the effective use of books and other materials as they are with making them available for public use. However, few public libraries actively seek to help users to develop their reading or study skills. Public libraries should consider joint initiatives with Adult Literacy and similar schemes, concerned with the development of new approaches to the provision of help with library skills, reading skills, and independent study skills for new readers and inexperienced learners. Developments at this end of the spectrum may also generate ideas which would be relevant to a wider range of library users.

- The library service should encourage members of the public to develop their reading and study skills
- The library should have books in stock on reading and study skills and audio-visual self-instructional materials dealing with these skills
- Arrangements should be made for library staff either to provide direct assistance for individuals or groups seeking to improve their skills or to refer them to other suitable agencies.

4.6.5 Help from subject specialists

Some large urban libraries which have specialist departments staffed by subject experts will be able to offer a range of specialist advice, provided directly by library staff themselves. Many other libraries—including most smaller libraries—are staffed by generalists. It is therefore important to consider other possible arrangements for providing access to help and advice from subject specialists, where this is what independent learners require (see also sections 4.3.5 and 4.3.6 above). Some of the main alternatives might include:

(a) Direct provision of subject specialist advice via library staff
(b) Identification of a 'panel' of voluntary subject specialists to whom learners may be referred, or who are willing to offer their services in the library
(c) Co-operative arrangements with a local education institution (university, polytechnic, college, adult education organization etc.) involving timetabled arrangements when subject specialists are available.

For subjects of popular interest it may sometimes also be worth considering special sessions in the library when a well-known expert would be available to answer questions, give advice and recommend appropriate books, etc.

− The subject specialist expertise which currently exists amongst the library staff should first be established
− The arrangements for gaining access to subject specialist advice should be publicized among library readers and the general public.

4.6.6 Help with keeping records of work

Most librarians would regard it as the business of the independent learner rather than the business of the library to keep a record of reading and work undertaken−and independent learners should normally be encouraged to do this for themselves.

However, the compilation of 'profile cards' on, for example, housebound readers suggests that this sort of arrangement can be useful for particular kinds of library users. Moreover, the computerization of library systems should make the extraction of information about previous borrowing a relatively easy matter− thereby enabling staff to make more intelligent recommendations for further reading. Clearly this is not a service to force on users, and there are questions of confidentiality to be considered. But where independent learners would regard such record keeping as helpful, it would seem to be a useful service to offer.

4.7 Summary of main recommendations

Each public library authority should:

(a) produce a development plan for meeting the needs of independent learners (4.2.1)

(b) assign to a senior member of staff responsibility for developing this service (4.2.1)

(c) ensure that all library staff are aware of the needs of independent learners, and adopt training programmes designed to help staff improve their assistance to learners (4.2.2)

(d) be able to provide information about a wide range of learning materials, including audio-visual and non-book materials (4.4.3)

(e) carry adequate information about educative broadcasting and related materials (4.4.4)

(f) provide information about local people and organizations able to offer assistance to independent learners (4.4.5, 4.4.6)

(g) participate in the development and running of any local educational guidance service for adults, and ensure that such a service gives adequate weight to independent learning opportunities (4.4.7)

(h) publicize (to the general public) its own stock and its services to adult independent learners (4.5.1)

(j) provide access to a comprehensive range of self-instructional materials, open learning packages, audio-visual and broadcast materials and hardware (4.5.2−5)

(k) provide study and meeting facilities for individuals and groups engaged in independent learning (4.5.6)

(l) offer appropriate guidance and support services for independent learners, e.g. help with planning learning (4.6.1), help with selecting materials (4.6.2), training to use the library more effectively (4.6.3), and help with reading and study skills (4.6.4).

4.8 Institutional sources of information relating to Chapter 4

4.4.3

Concord Films Council, 201 Felixstowe Road, Ipswich, Suffolk IP3 9BJ

Guild Film Library, Guild House, Peterborough PE2 9PZ.

4.4.4

TV Take up, available from the Programme Support and Development Group, IBA, 70 Brompton Road, London SW3 1EY

See 4, available from the Education Liaison Officer, Channel 4, 60 Charlotte Street, London W1P 2AX.

Other Channel 4 publications are available from Channel 4, PO Box 4000, London W3 6XJ or Glasgow G12 9JQ, or Belfast BT2 7FE.

BBC Education Newsletters are available from BBC Continuing Education, London W5 2PA.

Broadcast Support Services, 252 Western Avenue, London W3 6XJ

Educational Guidance Services for Adults, Room 208, Bryson House, 28 Bedford Street, Belfast BT2 7FE.

NETWORK Scotland Ltd., 74 Victoria Crescent Road, Glasgow G12 9JQ.

4.5.3

National Interactive Video Centre, 27 Marylebone Road, London NW1 5JS.

4.5.4

The Independent Broadcasting Trust, 2 Ferdinand Place, London NW1 8EE.

4.9 **Sources of structured materials for independent learning**

ABC, Historic Publications, Oldhill, London Road, Dunstable, Bedfordshire.

Audio Forum, 31 Kensington Church Street, London W8 4LL.

British Self-Study Centre, Avon House, 360 Oxford Street, London W1N 0AY.

Celtic Revision Aids, 17–23 Nelson Way, Tuscam Trading Estate, Camberley, Surrey GU15 3EU.

Charles Letts, 77 Borough Road, London SE1 1DW (Letts Study Aids).

Heinemann Computers in Education Ltd., 22 Bedford Square, London WC1B 3HH.

John Murray, 50 Albemarle Street, London W1X 4BD (Success Studybooks; also the ILEA 'APRIL' and 'ILPAC' materials for A-level physics and chemistry.

HLL Publications, 1 Westbourne Place, Hove, Sussex BN3 4GN.

Linguaphone Institute, 209 Regent Street, London W1R 8AU.

Longman Group Resources Unit, 33–35 Tanner Row, York. (Wide range of small format materials suitable for independent learners.)

Macdonald and Evans (M and E Handbooks), Estover Road, Estover, Plymouth PL6 7PZ.

Macmillan Publishers, 4 Little Essex Street, London WC2R 3LF. (Macmillan Master Series).

National Extension College, 18 Brooklands Avenue, Cambridge CB2 2HN.

Open University Education Enterprises, 12 Cofferidge Close, Stony Stratford, Milton Keynes MK11 1BY. ('Complete catalogue of audio-visual materials' and 'Complete catalogue of study units'.)

Pan Books, Cavaye Place, London SW10 9PG. (Pan study aids.)

Pitmans Correspondence College, Worcester Road, Wimbledon, London SW19 4DS.

Rapid Results College, 27–37 St Georges Road, London SW19 4DS.

W. H. Allen, 44 Hill Street, London W1X 8LB. (Made simple books.)

Wiley and Sons, Baffins Lane, Chichester, Sussex PO19 1UD.

Wolsey Hall, 66 Banbury Road, Oxford OX2 6PR.

Open Tech materials are detailed in 'Open Tech Directory' available from the National Extension College (see above) and on-line via MARIS-NET, a Prestel Gateway system.

References

1 Smith, V., *Public libraries and adult independent learners: a report*, London, CET, 1987.
2 Carter, J. and Neale, B., *Education, information, libraries and learners*, Bradford, MCB University Press Ltd, 1985, 10.
3 *British national film and video catalogue*, London, British Film Institute.
4 National Institute of Adult Continuing Education, *Yearbook of adult continuing education 1986−7*, Leicester, NIACE, 1986.
5 Unit for the Development of Adult Continuing Education, *The challenge of change: developing educational guidance for adults*, Leicester, NIACE, 1986.
6 The British Universities Film and Video Council, *Distributors index 1986*, London, BUFVC, 1986.

Further bibliography

Allred, J. and Hay, W., *A preliminary study of the involvement of public libraries with adult learners*, Leeds, Leeds Polytechnic, School of Librarianship, 1979.
Anderson, J. and Boyle, J., *Public libraries and educational broadcasting*, Penzance, Public Libraries Group of the Library Association, 1980.
Birge, E., *Serving adult learners: a public library tradition*, Chicago, American Library Association, 1981.
Brookfield, S. D., 'The adult learning iceberg: a critical review of the work of Allen Tough', *Adult education*, 54, 1981, 110−18.
Brookfield, S. D., *Adult learners, adult education and the community*, Milton Keynes, Open University Press, 1983.
Coleman, P. M., *Whose problem? the public library and the disadvantaged*, London, Association of Assistant Librarians, 1981.
Dale, S., 'Another way forward for adult learners: the public library and independent study', *Studies in adult education,* 12, (1), 1980, 29−38.
Drodge, S., *Adult education library provision*. Leicestershire, East Midlands Branch of the Library Association, 1984.
Heeks, P., *Library adult education: the unfulfilled promise*, Winchester, Public Libraries Research Group, 1982.

Lubans, J. (ed.), *Educating the public library user*, Chicago, American Library Association, 1983.

Monaco, J., 'Public libraries and adult independent learners: an action research programme', *Journal of community education*, **4**, (1), 1985, 14−20.

Percy, K. A. and Willett, I. H. (eds.), *Libraries and the future of adult education*, Lancaster, University of Lancaster, 1981.

Surridge, R. and Bowen, J., *The independent learning project: a study of changing attitudes in American public libraries*, Brighton, Public Libraries Research Group, 1977.

Tough, A., *The adult's learning projects*, Toronto, Ontario Institute for Studies in Education, 1971.

5 PUBLIC LIBRARIES AND ADULT STUDENTS

5.1 Scope

This chapter is concerned with public library services to adults who are (or intend to be) formally enrolled on courses of study. The nature and scope of formal continuing education have been outlined in sections 2.2.3–12, and the library needs of adult students have been described in sections 2.2.13–17. The present section deals with these needs under the same headings–educational information and guidance, library education and study skills, and access to library materials and facilities–with the one addition of training and collaboration.

5.2 Constraints

Because of the fragmented nature of adult education, librarians themselves have not always been aware of the full range of educational provision for adults, and a coherent policy in this area has often been difficult. At the same time an effective service to adult education requires a great deal of collaboration with local institutions, which in turn requires the regular use of staff time and resources. The latter constraint may be the main reason why many library authorities have not identified adult education (or indeed 'academic students' of any age[1] as a high priority area. And those authorities which have taken a conscious decision to be more involved in it, have usually confined themselves to the provision of educational information. There is therefore much more that can be done under our three main headings.

5.3 Educational information

The public library has traditionally provided information about local events for the general public. In particular it is one of the main sources of information for adults contemplating a formal course of study in the locality. Information about education provision at regional and national levels will also be required by many adults.

It is recommended that each public library authority should:

(a) maintain and display (centrally and at all branches) up-to-date collections of the publicity leaflets, brochures and posters of local adult education agencies, and the prospectuses of other local institutions offering courses for adults. This will involve a system of regular liaison with the agencies concerned

(b) participate in, or be a major component of, a local Educational Guidance Unit, a primary function of which will be to provide access to local and national educational information (see also 4.4.7). If a local unit has not been established, the public library should play a leading part in setting one up. Such a unit should maintain a computerized database of local information and should provide on-line access to such national databases as The Educational Counselling and Credit Transfer Information Service (ECCTIS) and the Professional, Industrial and Commercial Updating Programme (PICKUP) Short Course Directory

(c) formulate a policy on its role in any other educational information networks. A recent example is the Manpower Services Commission's Training Access Points (TAP) Unit, which is aiming to develop training opportunities information databases (to be accessible at strategic points in local communities)

(d) assign to a senior member of staff responsibility for the library's educational information service for adults. He should in turn designate members of staff to be responsible for operating the service at each branch

(e) publicize its educational information service among the general public.

5.4 Educational guidance

This is normally used as an umbrella term to include the provision of educational information, advice, counselling, assessment, and implementation. In the present context, however, it is confined to the provision of information and advice. Advising is defined as 'helping clients to interpret information and choose the most appropriate option'.[2]

The evidence suggests that many public librarians are reluctant to go beyond the role of information provider,[3] and the reasons include shortage of resources, and worry about a possible extension into the counselling role. However, public librarians have traditionally offered a service of information provision and interpretation as part of their daily routine. Advice to users is a natural extension of this, and it parallels the help given to independent learners in selecting materials and planning projects (see 4.6.1 and 4.6.2). But it is unrealistic to expect public library staff to be personally involved in the process of guidance beyond this point.

It is therefore recommended that each public library authority should:

(a) formulate and implement a policy for the provision of educational advice to adults, either through the library service or through the local Educational Guidance Unit, or through both
(b) arrange for the training of selected staff in the techniques of educational advice. UDACE has developed packages of training materials for this purpose
(c) publicize its educational advice service. Consideration should be given to the holding of exhibitions of adult education materials, and to enrolment periods (for local institutions) on library premises.

5.5 User education and the acquisition of study skills

The statements and recommendations already made in sections 4.6.3 and 4.6.4 (in the context of independent learning) apply here equally. In addition it is recommended that each public library authority should:

(a) encourage adult education tutors to take their students to the local library for introduction to the staff and familiarization with resources available
(b) arrange programmes of library instruction for local home-based students, especially those engaged on distance or open learning courses
(c) encourage library staff to participate in the planning and teaching of any locally-based courses concerned with study skills and the effective use of libraries.

5.6 Access to library materials and facilities

The library needs of adult students have already been outlined in sections 2.2.16 and 2.2.17. It should be emphasized again that the needs of individual students will vary considerably according to such factors as the type and level of the subjects and the location and length of the courses which they are pursuing. In general, however, adult students face considerable problems (e.g. access, time) in obtaining study materials. Public libraries, therefore, have a special responsibility to them and particularly to those who do not have easy access to institutional libraries. The aim of the following recommendations is to reduce the library-related problems of adults to a minimum.

(a) All adult education agencies and institutions should provide local public libraries with their course booklists and syllabuses, well before the beginning of the courses. This should include the booklists of national bodies, such as the Open University, which can be distributed regionally. Library staff should check as many booklists as possible against their own stocks, in anticipation of student demand. For some adult classes it will be helpful to inform tutors of the relevant library's holdings.

(b) Library staff should give bibliographical help to the teachers of adult courses when they are compiling their booklists.

(c) Libraries should provide book-boxes (special collections of books and other materials) for adult education courses at the class meeting-place, in appropriate cases. Appropriate cases normally include:

- University extramural courses offered by extramural departments which are too small to have their own library (see also 8.4.1)
- Other extramural courses where there is a special need for the university's book supply to be supplemented
- WEA courses, since the WEA has no library of its own
- LEA courses which are of an academic nature.

Such arrangements will involve close liaison with the organizing agencies.

(d) Libraries should make special purchases, including multiple copies of texts where appropriate, for the adult class provision described in (c).

(e) The library authority should build up a collection of audio-visual and other non-book materials suitable for use by adult education classes (both lecturers and students). Such materials should include slides, films, records and compact discs, audio and video tapes (including recorded broadcasts), video discs and computer software.

(f) Library staff should give advice, when requested, on how to make the most effective use of the materials listed in (e). In this context consideration should be given to the installation of computer terminals on library premises both for use by adult groups and for increasing computer literacy among the general public.

(g) Library staff should ensure that essential bibliographical aids and other reference materials are available for use by adult students in the central library and in branches.

(h) Library authorities should provide access to computerized literature searches (which may be of particular benefit to adult home-based students) and to computerized information services.

(j) Libraries should provide accommodation for adult education classes and study space for adult students. The former is particularly appropriate where it is necessary for the class to have direct access to the library's holdings (e.g. local history archives).

(k) Libraries should make available microfiche copies of their catalogues, and of union catalogues of networks, in adult education centres for use by students. Plans should begin for introducing access to on-line public library catalogues in non-library premises.

(l) Libraries should make special provision (of books and periodicals) for open learning students, by anticipating demand through regular contact with their tutors or institutions.

(m) Library staff should take note of the special needs of other adult students using the resources of the public library (e.g.

local part-time degree students, mature students at polytechnic or university) and try to meet these needs where appropriate.

(n) Libraries should make special provision for disadvantaged adult students, e.g. outreach services to the disabled or housebound, learning materials and 'reading clubs' for literacy students.

(o) Libraries should publicize their services to adult continuing education in special promotional material designed for circulation to educational institutions and to individual students.

5.7 Training and collaboration

One of the reasons why some public librarians have been reluctant to extend their role into services for adult education is the belief that the public library service exists for the general public and that it should not discriminate in favour of any particular group of people. One argument put forward in support of this belief is that everyone is a student in some sense, however formal or informal, so that the library service is already serving adult students as well as it can. However, this view ignores the fact that serving an individual student requires an assessment of needs and appropriate action to meet them, and that this is a kind of discrimination in his favour. In fact any kind of policy decision in a library has to involve some discrimination.

One of the main problems is that library staff are rarely familiar with the world of adult continuing education. Schools of librarianship should ensure that adult learners feature regularly as examples in the teaching of the management of library services. In practical terms there should be opportunities for public librarians to meet adult education administrators and tutors on a regular basis. The pattern set by the North West Public Libraries and Adult Education Committee should be adopted in other areas. Another possibility is for Regional Library Systems to expand their role to include all forms of co-operation between libraries and other relevant bodies; for example, the constitution of the West Midlands Regional Library System Executive Committee now allows for the co-option of a librarian to represent adult education interests.

(a) Libraries should assign to a senior member of staff responsibility for services to adult education.

(b) Library staff with responsibility for services to adult education should be familiar with how courses are created and with the aims and methods of adult education agencies.

(c) Formal links should be established and maintained between the public library service and adult education bodies. This may be done through a local co-ordinating committee or through the Regional Library System. In this way library staff and adult education practitioners will meet on a regular basis to discuss such issues as book supply, publicity, and accommodation.

(d) A co-ordinating committee should monitor the effectiveness of public library services to adult students in a locality and should initiate research projects into the library needs of adult students.

5.8 Summary of main recommendations

(a) Each public library should maintain and display the publicity materials for all local adult education providers (5.3).

(b) Each public library authority should participate in the work of a local Educational Guidance Unit. This participation should include the giving of educational advice (5.3, 5.4).

(c) Each public library authority should arrange programmes of library instruction for local adult classes and individual students (5.5).

(d) Public libraries should provide book-boxes for adult education classes, where appropriate (5.6).

(e) Public libraries should develop collections of non-book materials suitable for use by adult students and tutors (5.6).

(f) Public libraries should assign to a senior member of staff responsibility for services to adult education (5.7).

(g) Formal links should be maintained between the public library service and adult education bodies (5.7).

References

1 Barnett, C., 'Public libraries, students, and the provision of academic reading materials', in Baker, D. (ed.), *Student reading needs and higher education*, London, Library Association Publishing, 1986, 108–19.
2 Unit for the Development of Adult Continuing Education, *The challenge of change: developing educational guidance for adults*, Leicester, NIACE, 1986, 23–4.
3 Butler, L., *Educational guidance for adults: some terms, definitions and issues in the practice of educational guidance by independent services and public libraries*, ACACE, 1982, 45.

Further bibliography

Adult education and public libraries in the 1980's: a symposium, London, The Library Association, 1980.

Butler, L., *Information and technology in educational guidance for adults*, Leicester, UDACE, 1986.

Convention of Scottish Local Authorities, *Standards for the public library service in Scotland*, Edinburgh, COSLA, 1987.

Craig, R. and Gerver, E. (eds.), *Light in the darkness: Scottish libraries and adult education*, Edinburgh, Scottish Institute of Adult Education, 1985.

Public Libraries and Adult Education Committee for the North-West, *Guidelines for co-operation*, Liverpool, WEA West Lancashire and Cheshire District, 1978.

Turner, N., 'Libraries and community education', *Scottish journal of adult education*, **6**, (2), 1983, 23–7.

6 COLLEGE LIBRARIES AND ADULT STUDENTS

6.1 Introduction

College libraries work with adult learners in a wide variety of contexts. Not all of these are of equal significance, either in terms of number or in terms of the distinctiveness of provision which may need to be made specifically for adults. In particular there are clear overlaps in provision at the informal end of the spectrum (with public libraries—see chapters 4 and 5) and at the most formal end (with college libraries' own work in respect of mainstream taught courses—see the guidelines in *College libraries*[1]).

6.2 Scope

The term 'college' here refers primarily to colleges of further education and colleges of higher education.

In principle it is possible to envisage the provision by college libraries of every form of library service to every type of adult learner. Clearly this does not reflect reality. On the other hand, the fact that mature students on full-time courses are able to borrow books in the same way as their 16—19 year-old fellow-students is scarcely a distinctive form of provision. These guidelines therefore concentrate on those areas where college librarians do—or should—attempt to provide special services for adults, or where there is an area of controversy. The matrix overleaf sets out the possible range of provision, and indicates by a cross those covered in the text.

6.3 Access to library services

Whilst adult students on mainstream college courses will have automatic access to basic library services—bookstock, work area and equipment, reference services—this is not always the case for others. The college library should realistically be available not only to all registered college students, but to the local community as a whole, as a specialized tool of education.

	Access to library services	Library loans	Information skills	Study guidance/ learning support	Educational information
Mature f/t students			x		
Mature p/t students			x		
Attending MSC training		x	x		
Attending Access course		x	x		
Attending basic education	x	x	x		x
Non-vocational students	x	x	x		x
College open learners	x			x	x
Open University students	x			x	x
External open learners	x			x	x
Independent learners	x			x	x

6.3.1 This has implications for study space and, in particular, for the provision of work surfaces and seating. Ideally a small allowance for unattached learners should be added on to formula-related accommodation, and, more importantly, the weighting given to part-time students for the purposes of full-time equivalency needs to be adjusted upwards.

6.3.2 Many college libraries are not open every evening, and when they are open it is only until mid-evening, before the end of evening classes. In consequence evening class students can frequently not visit the library on the occasion of their class. Opening hours should cater for the needs of all students.

It follows that staffing is required outside the full-time course hours. Whenever possible qualified assistance should be available to library users.

6.3.3 A stock geared entirely to mainstream full- and part-time courses is likely to restrict the usefulness to many adult students of full access to the library. Whilst it would be unrealistic to expect everything ever taught in a college to be covered by the library, an analysis of the college programme permits stocking on the basis of those courses which run regularly.

6.4 Loan of library materials

Most adults likely to use the college library are part-time and/or short-term students. Others (those from categories 7–10 of the matrix) are not college-registered students at all (although some independent learners may be learning through community groups or clubs which are affiliated to the college in some way).

6.4.1 Part-time students, adult or otherwise, are entitled to full consideration in determining loans policy. In addition to the problem of stock alluded to in section 6.3.3, part-time students are particularly subject to disadvantage if they require materials in demand and kept in short loan collections. Where this is a problem action is required either to duplicate this stock for ordinary loan or to extend the short loan period to the period of frequency of part-time classes–usually one week.

6.4.1.1 Class collections or book boxes do make dedicated materials available for borrowing as well as easing the problems of access associated with restricted opening hours, and can be a useful approach. However, because they tie up stock whilst not permitting students a free range over possible materials, such as they would have through a visit to the library, they are best viewed as a good solution for classes at out-centres, but not on the main college site.

6.4.2 Short course students are often not allowed loans because of problems of recovery. It is preferable to use loans of shorter duration. Information about the exact length of courses is not always easy for the librarian to obtain, but is vital in order to administer this area adequately.

6.4.3 It is desirable for all adult learners to be able to borrow from the college library. Financial and resultant stock exigencies often mean that this is unrealistic, but the goal of service to the local community as a whole is a valid one, and college libraries may at least be able to make the case for funding to enable the service to be implemented.

6.5   Information skills instruction

Adult learners from all the matrix categories may benefit from instruction in information skills, but it is clear that those most likely to need extended and/or formal attention are those who wish to make the most extensive use of the library.

6.5.1   Particular candidates in this respect are those students who are spending a substantial amount of time in college. Firstly this means mature students attending 'mainstream' courses, who are likely to be attending for information/library skills sessions along with their younger fellow-students.

6.5.1.1   Just as some aspects of college full-time provision (e.g. physical education or elective studies) may be less appropriate to adults than to 16–19 year-olds, so elements of a standard information skills programme may have to be re-thought. Depending on the approach of local schools, it is often possible to assume (in the case of younger students) some prior instruction in information skills, but this is unlikely to be the case with adults. On the other hand, adults' experience in obtaining and using information for daily life–as opposed to study–is much wider than that of younger students.

6.5.1.2   In the context of general library instruction, which almost inevitably brings the whole class along together, it follows that what is the best practice for 16–19 information skills work is even more appropriate where adults are in the group: an activity-based approach, with a clear purpose, is not only more acceptable and effective, but also allows the librarian to spend time assisting individuals or small groups according to their needs. Where the information area is appropriate it will also allow the librarian to exploit the life experience of adults in the group by ensuring that they are not isolated, but working with younger students.

6.5.1.3   Adults can be acutely aware of their own shortcomings in basic study skills, of which information handling is one. It may be useful, therefore, to try to arrange a special session for mature students, where their lack of skills (real or presumed), as compared with students straight from school, will not be exposed. If this is impossible, or very difficult, an informal approach when students are using the library is the best substitute.

6.5.2 Some adults attending college regularly do so in the company only of other adults, so that adults-only sessions are automatic.

6.5.2.1 Whilst the range of educational backgrounds will vary considerably, it is likely that most adults attending college on Access or re-training courses, or particularly for basic education, will have limited information and other study skills. A programme for them must therefore cover basics, but without demeaning their status as mature people with real skills and experience of their own. Time permitting, it is best to start from the existing knowledge of class members, drawing out lessons from that, rather than commencing with a contents list.

6.5.2.2 Librarians are unlikely to have much contact with adult non-vocational students. Such students tend to have a higher previous educational base than the groups in section 6.5.2.1 and the best approach is likely to be a practical one, strictly subject-orientated and dealing solely with what the students need to know in order to use the library for what will generally be a fairly limited purpose.

6.5.3 Adults not attending the college on a regular basis may well use the library, but as individuals rather than as class members. In this case an information skills programme in any formal sense seems inappropriate. Their needs are more likely to be met through individual guidance (see section 6.6).

6.6 Student guidance/learning support
Any learner, whether or not an adult or attending a formal course, *may* turn to the librarian for assistance in actually planning and effecting his or her work. With adults attending taught courses,

however, this should be occasional, as the course tutor is the natural first assistant.

6.6.1 Detached or 'semi-detached' learners, i.e. independent learners or those engaged in open learning and non-formal education, are much more likely to need support beyond the librarian's traditional information role. Once these adults have made the decision to use the college library, the librarian largely becomes the college for them. As an academic, whether so designated or not, the librarian should try to respond to this.

6.6.1.1 It would be inappropriate for the role of college librarian to be so defined as to include the formal direction of complete learning programmes in this area, not least because formal direction is largely inimical to truly independent learning. Nevertheless, assisting an independent learner to analyse information acquired and to decide an appropriate sequence of study and appropriate selection of materials is in line with some public library developments (cf. section 4.6); college librarians have considerable experience of how, and with what success, their stock is used for study, and they will be able to extrapolate from this for the benefit of independent learners.

6.6.1.2 Open learning, resting upon learning resources of different varieties, needs some form of central base within a college, and it is natural for the college library to provide this. Whilst tutoring is the province of the subject specialist, the college library should be actively involved. This means not only the provision of a learning environment and access to open learning materials and equipment housed in the library, but also support for the learner in their use. Formal tutorial support is likely to be limited, so that it is invaluable for the learner to have assistance at least with dealing with the mechanisms of open learning packs which are to be used on site. The college librarian can offer this assistance by becoming familiar with the main packs provided.

6.7 Educational information

Information about educational opportunities is as natural a part of the college library's service as other areas of information and should be available as a matter of course for all users of the college.

6.7.1 This service should include not only the standard information about full-time and vocational courses, but also information about part-time and open learning opportunities. The obvious home in a college for such on-line services as MARIS-NET is the library.

6.8 Conclusions: staffing and funding implications

There are clear resource implications resulting from the foregoing recommendations, some of which have been alluded to already.

6.8.1 Any extension of opening hours implies an increase in staffing; if advice is to be offered, this means professionally trained staff.

6.8.2 The librarian's role described in this chapter is wider than the traditional one (although in line with what many college librarians already do). Training, particularly in guidance techniques, may be required.

6.8.3 Both accommodation and stock could be placed under severe pressure by the sort of use suggested here.

6.8.4 Open learning packs are often very expensive. If the college library acts as an open learning base specific funding will be needed for the base collection.

6.8.5 The use of such services as MARIS-NET is costly, particularly by small library standards. Special funding may be required.

6.8.6 Some support services may be provided at the direct or indirect behest of other institutions (particularly open learning support). In some cases the host institution may wish to charge the parent institution; in others the support may be deemed to be reciprocal. In either case it is the library which actually carries the burden, and this needs to be recognized in funding.

6.8.7   The less formal area of the matrix of learners has received particular attention above, despite the fact that this is likely to be a relatively small part of the total provision at the present time. This is in recognition of two factors: firstly that such learners might otherwise be overlooked; and secondly that current developments in further and adult education (e.g. the Open College) make this a crucial area for all colleges, in which their libraries cannot afford not to participate.

6.9   Summary of main recommendations

(a) The college library and its services should be available not only to all registered college students but to the local community as a whole (6.3).
(b) Opening hours and study space should cater for the needs of both part-time and full-time students (6.3.1, 6.3.2).
(c) Loans policy should take account of the needs of part-time and short-course students (6.4.1, 6.4.2).
(d) Library instruction programmes should include, and draw on the existing experience of, adult students (6.5.1, 6.5.2).
(e) Library staff should give guidance to independent learners in selecting materials and deciding an appropriate sequence of study (6.6.1.1).
(f) Library staff should assist open learning students in selecting and using open learning packs (6.6.1.2).
(g) The library should provide a full range of educational information (6.7).
(h) Library staffing and funding should be sufficient to support the additional materials and services implied in the above recommendations (6.8).

Reference

1 The Library Association, *College libraries: guidelines for*

professional service and resource provision, London, Library
Association, 3rd edn, 1982.

Further bibliography

Council for Educational Technology, *Learning resources in
colleges: their organization and management*, London, CET,
1981.
Latcham, J. and Kelly, L. U., *Open learning: an introductory
reading list*, Coombe Lodge, The Further Education Staff
College, 1986.
Open Learning Federation, *Newsletter* (3 a year), Barnet, Barnet
College.

7 POLYTECHNIC LIBRARIES AND ADULT STUDENTS

7.1 The polytechnics and continuing education

7.1.1 The 30 polytechnics in England and Wales have had a strong commitment to continuing education since their inception. From their early days, they have always had large numbers of part-time students, many of whom have been mature students.

7.1.2 Part-time students continue to form a large proportion of the student population in the polytechnics. About 40% of polytechnic enrolments are part-time students. Over half of these are mature students over the age of 25.

7.1.3 Continuing education is growing in importance in the polytechnics as they seek more adult students. Their pattern of educational provision is evolving to reflect changing needs and to cope with continuing financial stringency. Demographic trends arising from a decline in the birthrate means a less ready supply of home entrants into full-time higher education direct from school. This has been part of the motivation for many polytechnics to extend educational opportunities to those, such as older students, women, ethnic minorities, people from working-class backgrounds, and people with disabilities who have not been well catered for in the past.

7.1.4 In order to attract a broader range of applicants, however, the polytechnics are having to address themselves as to how students might be given more choice in the pattern of delivery of courses (e.g. through more opportunities for part-time study, through the development of distance learning courses, through 'credit transfer' to allow movement between institutions, through self-paced study packages, or through independent learning in which the student negotiates a 'learning contract'). It has also led to a reappraisal of entry qualifications and, particularly, the growth of 'Access courses' (usually with neighbouring further education colleges) aimed at people who are unaccustomed to study and who need a gateway into the higher education system.

7.1.5 At the same time, there is a strong demand for post-experience professional and vocational courses from those who wish to keep abreast of technological and other change. This need is being met in the polytechnics through short courses, mainly directed at the needs of local industry, and through the development of part-time postgraduate courses.

7.1.6 One of the effects of the polytechnics' commitment to continuing education is a diversification in the composition of the student population. It is no longer possible to view the 'normal' student as a full-time student who has entered the polytechnic straight from school. Such students are already in the minority in some polytechnics and are likely to become so in others.

7.2 Polytechnic library services and continuing education

7.2.1 Availability of library services

7.2.1.1 The full services of the polytechnic library should be available to all students who have enrolled at the polytechnic irrespective of their mode of attendance or the duration of the course. This includes part-time students, students on access courses at the polytechnic, short course students, and students on distance learning courses.

7.2.1.2 Polytechnic libraries should examine closely their policies which exclude external readers from reference facilities to see whether they are really necessary to protect their own readers. A charge might be made for borrowing rights for external students. The library, like any other part of the polytechnic, has a role in promoting the polytechnic as an institution and in marketing its educational services. External readers who receive a welcoming approach from the polytechnic library are likely to build up a positive image of the polytechnic. Every external reader is a potential student in the future. Libraries with special collections, such as the Fawcett Library on women's issues at the City of London Polytechnic, have particular opportunities and obligations in respect of external readers.

7.2.1.3 Particular efforts should be made for students on Access courses at neighbouring further education colleges. The polytechnic library needs to build close links with the libraries where these courses are run, be prepared to offer the students use of the polytechnic library, and provide familiarization tours.

7.2.2 Developing and marketing services

7.2.2.1 The composition of the student population is becoming more diverse as more adult students are attracted into the polytechnics. No one approach to library provision is going to meet the needs of all students. Polytechnic libraries need to recognize this diversity and develop services to meet the needs of clearly defined sub-groups of the student body. Library services and their promotion need to be tailored to meet specific needs.

7.2.2.2 Polytechnic libraries do not have a captive market for their services amongst many non-traditional students. It cannot be assumed that part-time students and short course students are aware that they are entitled to use the library. Furthermore, if the library is not providing what these students require, or is perceived not to do so, the students are more likely to use other libraries or buy their books than their full-time counterparts. As a basis for remedial action, libraries should monitor levels of library usage by part-time students and short-course students to ascertain which groups of students are using the library, which are not, and which are under-utilizing it. Bristol and City of London Polytechnics have used automated circulation systems to provide information on market penetration.

7.2.2.3 Part-time students and short course students, by their very nature, will tend to visit the library less frequently than full-timers. Students on distance courses may never visit it. It will involve a special effort on the part of the library to ascertain the needs of those who use the library infrequently or not at all. Libraries must develop ways of obtaining the views of non-traditional students on their need for and use of library services. This could mean undertaking questionnaire surveys, group discussions, or depth interviews amongst targeted segments of the user population. Levels of participation might be low amongst students who have limited time or who may not perceive the value of the library. It could involve 'outreach' work where library staff purposively seek to talk to students at teabreaks or through 'library stalls' located in student common rooms, through contact with the mature students' association, or through 'library open days'.

7.2.2.4   Ideas for improving library access and service delivery can be generated in brainstorming sessions where library staff suggest different ways of providing services to meet the special needs of different groups. The ideas which arise can then be assessed as to their practicality.

7.2.2.5   Some initiatives may be of benefit to relatively small numbers of students but they should not be discarded if the costs are not great and they are of value to the few who benefit.

7.2.2.6   Publicity about the library should be distributed to all continuing education students. It should be well designed and aimed at specific sections of the user population. It should advertise services which are particularly relevant to that group. Newcastle-upon-Tyne Polytechnic and the Polytechnic of North London, for example, both produce such leaflets aimed at students on evening-only courses. City of London Polytechnic distributes a leaflet via its registry to part-time students based at its Moorgate site. Libraries might consider a library newsletter specifically aimed at continuing education students which addresses itself to the difficulties faced by adult students in studying and using libraries.

7.2.2.7 Any new initiatives should be carefully monitored to assess their success (although the criteria for success are rarely simple). It must be remembered though that new services must be given sufficient time to become established and not prematurely withdrawn.

7.2.3 Supporting and encouraging polytechnic initiatives

7.2.3.1 Library staff need to work closely with staff who are developing part-time courses, short courses, or distance courses. Lecturers need to be convinced themselves of the usefulness and relevance of the library so that these attitudes may then be passed on to their students. Subject librarians should have an active role in the development of courses and give the fullest guidance to teaching staff on how library resources might be used to enhance students' learning. There is a danger that increased choice for students in pace and location of study, through the development of self-contained packages, may be at the expense of choice of learning materials to suit different learning styles. Liaison with part-time teaching staff is particularly important as their contact with the polytechnic may be as restricted as their students.

7.2.3.2 The library also needs to have good contacts with registry and administrative staff so that the library is routinely informed of students who have special educational needs. This might include those who are disabled, visually handicapped, or dyslexic. The library should then respond positively to their special requirements. The library also needs to be informed about direct entry or 'credit transfer' students who enter the polytechnic in the second year of a course and will need some library orientation and instruction..

7.2.3.3 The library must be actively associated with the polytechnic's initiatives on continuing education. This means participation in relevant committees or working parties (such as those on open learning at Newcastle-upon-Tyne Polytechnic and the Polytechnic of North London). It could involve the collection of information on continuing education, open learning, and the study problems faced by mature students and its dissemination to teaching and administrative staff. At Newcastle-upon-Tyne, this includes collecting information on sources of funding for open learning schemes and developing links with award giving bodies.

7.2.3.4 The library is a 'shopwindow' for the polytechnic. The library is often located in a central location or on the ground floor of buildings. It is open longer hours than most other parts of the polytechnic. It has professional staff who are trained in enquiry work. There is no reason why the library should not take on the role of a referral centre for information about learning opportunities within the polytechnic. It could also be the 'gatekeeper' between outside callers and their need for information, consultancy, or training from within the polytechnic. A model of such a development is Hertis Information for Industry based at Hatfield Polytechnic.

7.2.3.5 The library has a unique role in providing greater choice to students in the range of learning materials which they might use in their learning. Libraries have printed works, videos, audiocassettes, and computer software to suit differing learning styles and special learning needs. Polytechnics should be made aware of this unique contribution to open learning. Libraries could distribute video or audio productions of lectures to increase students' choice in time of study.

7.2.4   Improving access to library resources

7.2.4.1 Continuing education students are more likely to face conflicting pressures on their time than traditional full-time students. Many part-time students are in paid or unpaid work. Much of their time at the polytechnic will be taken up in classes. Many mature students have family and childcare responsibilities. Opportunities for continuing education students to use the library are usually much more limited than for traditional students.

7.2.4.2 Libraries should look at extending opening hours as a measure to particularly benefit part-time students. Saturday or

Sunday opening is likely to be helpful to evening students. Serious attention should be given to ways in which some form of weekend opening might be provided even if the services offered are limited or availability is restricted to the weeks before examinations. Vacation evening opening is likely to be of value to part-timers who are unlikely to distinguish vacation from termtime in such a marked way as full-time students. Evening opening may also be needed for students on short courses or summer schools which are run in the vacations. Library opening though needs to be backed up with the availability of refectory and creche facilities.

7.2.4.3 Part-time students and short-course students are unlikely to visit the library frequently or for very long. They will face particular problems in orientating themselves in the library and finding what they want because of their unfamiliarity with the library layout and library systems. Mature students may lack confidence in studying and using large academic libraries. Sufficient library staff should be on hand at those times when non-traditional students are most likely to use the library to assist students on a one-to-one basis. Library skills, possibly linked with other information handling skills (especially study skills), should be incorporated into course design wherever appropriate. Pre-publicized voluntary tours of the library might be offered or a workbook approach involving independent study could be adopted. Audio-visual materials describing library facilities and how to use them could be produced for showing in classes or for independent study. Videos in a VHS format could even be loaned for home viewing. Microcomputer packages might be developed to assist students find their way around the library.

7.2.4.4 Consideration might be given to a special telephone service or 'Library line' by which non-traditional students might be given advice on using the library, obtain an enquiry service, and might order or reserve materials needed for their courses. Newcastle-upon-Tyne Polytechnic provides a telephone service for evening students of this kind. Libraries with an interactive catalogue on the polytechnic network might be able to provide on-line access in those classrooms frequently used by part-time students. It might also be possible to provide dial-up access for those students with the appropriate equipment at home or at work. Students could in this way search the library catalogue, check upon the availability of items, and order those items required.

7.2.4.5 A postal loan service should be provided for students on distance courses. Postal loans might also be considered for part-time students on courses where there are few opportunities or no opportunity at all for visiting the library. Alternatively, book boxes containing recommended texts could be deposited with classes under the supervision of teaching staff. More radical solutions could involve librarians and academic staff collaborating in making collections of reading available in printed, microfiche, or even electronic, formats. Microfiche has been successfully used for law students at Bristol Polytechnic. Copyright clearance is obviously required for producing such collections.

7.2.4.6 Students on part-time courses are often competing with their full-time counterparts for the same books. This is particularly true when courses are run concurrently in full-time and part-time modes. As full-time students have more opportunities to visit the library, part-time students tend to be disadvantaged. Libraries might consider creating a special textbook collection for part-time students (such as those set up at South Bank Polytechnic and Sheffield Polytechnic). It has been found at City of London Polytechnic that neither purchasing more duplicate copies of texts nor reducing the loan length of texts particularly assists part-time students when they are in competition for the same books with full-time students. Lecturers might be encouraged to provide longer reading lists to relieve the intensity of pressure but students will need additional guidance on what is essential reading and what is background reading.

7.2.4.7 Libraries might consider variable loan lengths for different groups of students. Short-loan collections are of little use to part-time students who have limited opportunities to consult items in the library and are likely to attend the polytechnic only once a week. It might be possible, for example, to lend short loan items for a week to part-time students. Distance students might need to borrow books for longer periods if they are dependent on a postal loan service. Full-time mature students with childcare responsibilities may experience difficulties in using short loan collections which do not permit overnight borrowing before 4 p.m. or 5 p.m. Non-traditional students might be allowed to borrow more items on the basis that they are more likely to want to use materials outside the library.

7.2.4.8 Non-traditional students will tend to make use of more than one library for their study. They generally live further away from the polytechnic and they visit the polytechnic less frequently. This argues for close co-operation between libraries. This might include the negotiation of access between academic libraries for each others' students. City of London Polytechnic, for example, has bilateral agreements with the North-East London Polytechnic, Polytechnic of Central London, and Thames Polytechnic to allow part-time students reciprocal borrowing facilities. Printed guides of local library facilities might be produced. The Polytechnic of North London, for example, produces a leaflet listing local public libraries open on Saturdays. It is important that students are taught to use libraries and information generally, not just their own polytechnic library. Such an approach will also benefit the increasing number of students who will study at more than one institution as a result of 'credit transfer'.

7.2.5 Diverting resources to continuing education students

7.2.5.1 Polytechnic library services have been largely developed with the needs of traditional full-time students in mind. It will take strong leadership and political will to achieve a transfer of resources away from full-time students to other groups of students especially in the context of the tight resource constraints faced by most polytechnic libraries. It is important that the polytechnic is made fully aware of the additional library costs of providing effective services to non-traditional students and that the problem is not entirely 'owned' by the library.

7.2.5.2 Financial allocation to libraries tends to be on the basis of FTEs (full-time equivalent student numbers). In many of these calculations, part-time students and short course students are very lowly weighted and do not adequately reflect the costs of library provision. Some part-time courses, particularly at post-graduate level, are more dependent on library use and more costly to support than some full-time courses. There are extra costs arising from higher levels of non-return of books by students on non-traditional courses.

7.2.5.3 Libraries might argue for a proportion of the money derived from the fees of part-time and continuing education students to be handed over to the library. For courses which are run on a full cost-recovery basis, the library needs to make an assessment of the costs of library provision and this should be included in the course fees.

7.2.6 Library staff development

7.2.6.1 A considerable rethink about library access and service delivery is necessary to ensure that polytechnic libraries respond positively to the continuing education initiatives in the polytechnics and the needs of a much broader user population. A key element in all of this will be the attitudes of library staff. Staff development may be required to encourage a positive attitude to these developments and to develop new skills to meet the challenge.

7.2.7 Summary of main recommendations
(a) The full service of the polytechnic library should be available to all students who have enrolled at the polytechnic irrespective of their mode of attendance or the duration of the course (7.2.1.1).
(b) Libraries must develop ways of obtaining the views of non-traditional students on their need for and use of library services, and should monitor usage of the library by specific groups of continuing education students (7.2.2.2−3).
(c) Library staff should work closely with those teaching and

administrative staff who are concerned with continuing education courses, and should support polytechnic initiatives in continuing education (7.2.3.1—5).

(d) Library opening hours should be extended for the benefit of part-time students (7.2.4.2).

(e) The acquisition of library skills should be regarded as a particular need of part-time students and should be incorporated into course design wherever appropriate (7.2.4.3).

(f) Libraries should consider creating special textbook collections for part-time students and variable loan lengths for different groups of students (7.2.4.6—7).

(g) The additional costs of providing effective library services to non-traditional students should be recognized by the polytechnic and adequate funds should be allocated (7.2.5.1—3).

Further reading

Bevan, N., 'Library services and the part-time student', in Fletcher, J. (ed.), *Reader services in polytechnic libraries*, Aldershot, Gower in association with COPOL, 1985, 159—83.

Blagden, P., *The library needs of part-time students preparing for professional examinations*, (Library Research Digest No.10), London, City of London Polytechnic, LRRS Publications, 1984.

Library Association, University College and Research Section, *Open learning and its impact on academic libraries*, (UC & R Discussion Paper No. 2), Nottingham, Library Association, University College and Research Section, 1985.

McDowell, E., *Part-time students and libraries: the results of research studies at Newcastle-upon-Tyne Polytechnic Library*, Newcastle-upon-Tyne, Newcastle-upon-Tyne Polytechnic Products Ltd, 1985.

Payne, P. (ed.), *The part-time student in the library: papers prepared for a conference held at City of London Polytechnic, April 15th and 16th, 1982*, London, LLRS Publications, 1983.

8 UNIVERSITY LIBRARIES AND ADULT STUDENTS

8.1 Introduction

The steady increase in recent years in the number of adults pursuing university courses of various kinds has led to a wider range of non-traditional patterns of study. This has created new problems for university libraries, problems relating to access, membership, special services, and the allocation of resources. However, because these changes have been relatively slow, and because the ratio of part-time to full-time students in the university sector is still low, many university librarians have paid little or no attention to the problems. Financial pressures are also to blame: the level of inflation for academic books and periodicals is much higher than for any other items of university expenditure, and this fact would seem to leave little room for changes in policy, apart from cuts in purchases.

Another complication is that the structural pattern of library services for continuing education students, as far as they exist, varies among universities, as does that of services for full-time internal students. At some the emphasis is on centralization, at others there is more devolution, with services being provided by a range of specialized departmental libraries as well as by the main library. These differences in structure usually bear little relationship to the various needs of adult students. For these many reasons, then, there is a clear need for general guidelines in this area.

8.2 Scope

This chapter deals with the library services provided by universities for those adults who are (or intend to be) enrolled on university courses. Within this category come post-experience courses, extramural and external courses, and part-time degree and diploma courses.

Also included are mature students (many of whom in lacking

formal matriculation qualifications have been accepted for university through a special scheme of mature matriculation) and adult independent learners. Some general guidelines, based on resources and services, are given first (section 8.3) followed by some more specific guidelines based on different types of courses and the different types of libraries within universities (section 8.4).

8.3 General guidelines

8.3.1 Planning
A university should assume full responsibility for the library services to its continuing education courses. A university which offers a programme of continuing education courses for adults should attempt to identify the library and information needs of its adult students, and of the relevant teaching staff, on a continuous basis. This should be done by regular surveys. Whenever a new course is proposed, the library resource implications should be considered at an early stage in the planning process and a written statement of the course needs should be prepared. The planning process should involve library staff as well as academic teaching staff. The appropriate on-campus library (main library, departmental, extramural, etc.) should be assigned the responsibility for meeting the stated needs of each course.

8.3.2 Finance
A university should provide regular financial support, as part of its annual budget, for library services to continuing education courses. The fund for books, and that for materials and services, should be calculated for part-time students on the same basis (pro-rata) as for full-time students. The most appropriate measure in this context is the number of student contact hours. Each library servicing continuing education courses should be assigned its fund on this basis. In addition, funds may be required for the contractual arrangements (for home-based independent students) with other libraries in the region.

8.3.3 The University Librarian should have continuous oversight of all library services to continuing education courses, whether he or she is directly responsible for them or not (see 8.3.1 above). In addition, each on-campus library providing such a service should have at least one professional librarian employed to plan and implement the service from that library. Professional staff are required for budget control, the allocation of resources, liaison with academic teaching staff and collaboration with adult education agencies. The total number of professional staff required for on-campus continuing education courses should be determined by the number of student contact hours involved (on the same basis as the book-fund). When the scale of operations is sufficiently large, the librarian in charge of the service to continuing education should be on the academic-related salary scales. Sufficient numbers of non-professional staff (library assistants, clerical and technical) should be employed to enable the service to be effective.

8.3.4 Resources

The main objective of the library service should be immediacy of access to required materials by adult students, wherever their class is located. This may involve delivery to off-campus locations, the establishment of off-campus study centres, or the provision of deposit collections in on-campus classrooms. It will certainly involve a well-planned but flexible system for the submission of requests to the libraries concerned and for the rapid supply of material needed. Core collections representing the main subject areas taught in continuing education classes should be built up. A major feature of these will be multiple copies of standard texts.

These core collections, reserved for the use of continuing education students, should be seen as largely superseding the traditional short-loan collections, which are rarely of much practical use to part-time adult students.

Where there are several departmental libraries on a campus serving various continuing education courses, it will be necessary to ensure that the degree of duplication of stock among them is not excessive.

Where the scale of operations is sufficiently large, a separate library should be established to serve off-campus or extramural courses (see 8.4.1).

8.3.5 Services and facilities

In serving continuing education students each university should participate in, and contribute financially to, the local Educational Guidance Unit.

Each university main library, and its departmental libraries where appropriate, should:

(a) provide information about educational opportunites for adults
(b) ensure that library opening hours are such that adult students (especially evening class students) are not denied access at times which are reasonably suitable to themselves
(c) arrange user education programmes specially designed for adults who are returning to study after a period of time, or entering higher education for the first time
(d) offer bibliographical services (including computerized literature searches where needed) to adult students
(e) offer assistance with non-print media and equipment to adult students
(f) ensure that adult students have access to facilities such as photocopying and inter-library loans
(g) ensure that adult students have access to library catalogues, both on-campus and off-campus (e.g. through study centres, public libraries)
(h) take account of the needs of adult students when developing services involving new technology (e.g. document facsimile transmission, interactive video discs, CD-ROM)
(j) grant full library membership, where needed, to those part-time (university course) tutors who are not members of the university (normally to be effective only for the tutor's period of engagement)
(k) grant full library membership to all part-time adult students who are enrolled on award-bearing courses arranged by the university, whether internal or external
(l) grant full library membership, for a fee, to those members of the general public who are not members of the university but who are engaged in a scholarly pursuit on a long-term basis

requiring use of an academic library; this policy should include Open University and London University external degree students (and any others of similar status), preferably by contractual arrangement with the parent institutions

(m) maintain a policy of free access (for reference purposes only) for those members of the public who have a genuine need on a short-term basis to use the university's library resources; this policy might include special provision for adult independent learners (as defined in 4.1)

(n) publicize library services for part-time and external adult students in the appropriate library guides.

8.4 Types of courses

As already stated, there are many different ways in which adults can participate in university-level education. The following are the categories of courses involved, but it should be pointed out that these are not necessarily mutually exclusive, nor is the list comprehensive.

8.4.1 Extramural courses

These are part-time courses arranged by university departments of extramural studies or their equivalent (i.e. of those universities which are Responsible Bodies and receive DES grant for this purpose). The majority of these courses are 'liberal adult education' for the general public not leading to a named qualification but of a sufficiently high academic standard to require a certain level of library support. A smaller proportion are in the category of professional or role education, and some of these are not grant-aided.

It is recommended that both these categories of courses (which may be either on-campus or off-campus) should, where the scale of operation justifies it, be supported by a separate extramural library service, i.e. a library dedicated solely to the needs of extramural students and tutors. The main function of such libraries should be for the supply of special collections of books and other materials to adult classes, and a supporting audio-visual service for tutors. Direct borrowing facilities may also be necessary for some on-campus courses.

Such libraries may be financed by the University Library or by the Department of Extramural Studies or its equivalent (or by a combination of the two); but the main allegiance should be to the Department and there should be close collaboration with its academic teaching staff.

Recommended minimum standards for extramural libraries have already been formulated,[1] and these are still applicable. The main recommendations are concerned with minimum annual book-funds, an average minimum of books to be supplied per course, and control of the library's academic and professional standards (by a full-time professional academic-related librarian).

Where an extramural department serves a small population and arranges a small programme of courses, it is the responsibility of the university to make alternative arrangements for library support. This should preferably take the form of a direct service from the local public library systems (by contractual agreement), or, failing this, an alternative extramural service from the university main library.

The emphasis throughout should be in the provision of reading materials at the class meeting-place, so that books can be immediately available and so that reading can play an integral part in the process of learning.[2]

Most liberal adult education courses should, therefore, receive an adequate service from the university's extramural library; and because most extramural students live or work some distance from the university, full membership of the university library (for direct borrowing) is neither necessary nor practical. However, some extramural courses are award-bearing; these require a wider library provision and warrant full membership (see 8.4.3 and 8.4.4).

8.4.2 Post-experience courses

These are the short vocational education courses provided by universities and offered mainly by the appropriate subject departments (i.e. not by extramural departments). They range in length from one day to several months and may be part-time or full-time; most are on-campus, a few are off-campus.

Students attending these courses are the responsibility of the university department which arranged their course, and they should have access to the appropriate departmental libraries. Very short, concentrated courses will require few, if any, library resources. Again, it is not necessary or practical for all post-experience students to have full membership rights at a university main library. However, such rights will be necessary for some longer courses (e.g. full-time courses of six weeks or more). It would seem sensible to treat each course on its merits, and university libraries should adopt a policy of granting full membership where there is a clearly defined need, for the duration of the course.

8.4.3 Part-time degree courses

Adult students pursuing degree courses through attending part-time evening classes on campus have library needs similar to full-time undergraduates but considerably more problems in satisfying these needs. Full borrowing rights at the university library should be granted (see 8.3.5, (k)), but there will still be problems relating to opening hours (see 8.3.5, (b)), use of short-loan collections, and competition with full-time students for heavy-demand titles. These problems should be alleviated by the provision of special collections of library materials (ideally deposited in the classroom) by the extramural library or by the university library (see 8.3.4).

Adult students pursuing external degree courses through home-based independent study, or through distance-teaching methods, should be granted borrowing rights at their local university library (see 8.3.5, (l)). This should be arranged on the basis of an annual charge payable by the home institution. In addition a direct mailing service to individual students based on a stock which has been developed specifically for this purpose, should be provided by their own university library. There should also be close collaboration with public libraries concerning the needs of independent degree students.

8.4.4 Certificate and diploma courses

Several universities offer a range of courses leading to named qualifications other than degrees. When these courses are arranged by the extramural department, the library needs should be treated as for 'Extramural courses' above; otherwise they should be treated in the same way as 'Post-experience courses'.

8.5 Summary of main recommendations

(a) A university should assume full responsibility for the library services to its continuing education courses (8.3.1) and provide regular financial support for them (8.3.2).

(b) The appropriate on-campus library should be assigned responsibility for meeting the needs of each course (8.3.1), with a professional librarian responsible for this activity at each library (8.3.3).

(c) Core collections, reserved for the use of continuing education students, should be built up (8.3.4).

(d) A university library should formulate, and carry out, a policy of special services to its adult students, particularly in relation to opening hours, user education and access to catalogues (8.3.5).

(e) A university should grant library membership (for a fee) to the local home-based external degree students of other institutions (8.3.5 and 8.4.3).

(f) Extramural courses should normally be served by a separate extramural library, concentrating on the supply of special collections to off-campus locations (8.4.1).

References

1 The Library Association, *Standards for university extramural libraries*, London, LA, 1978.

2 Bailey, R. H., 'What's all this about university standards?', *Adult education*, **59**, (3), 1986, 227–32.

Further bibliography

Association of College and Research Libraries, 'Guidelines for extended campus library services', *College and research libraries news*, **43**, (3), 1982, 86–8.

Brockman, J. R. and Klobas, J. E., *Libraries and books in distance education*, Perth, Western Australia Institute of Technology, 1983.

Davies, J. H., 'Adults and reading', in Thorton, A. H. and Stephens, M. D. (eds.), *The university in its region*, University of Nottingham, Department of Adult Education, 1977, 100−9.

Fisher, R. K., 'Library services for university adult education: a neglected area', *Adult education*, **53**, (6), 1981, 372−5.

Fisher, R. K., *The libraries of university departments of adult education and extramural studies*, (LA pamphlet 36), London, Library Association, 1974.

Fisher, R. K., *Library services to university extension students in the USA*, London, British Library Research and Development Department (report no. 5432), 1978.

Gains, D., 'Libraries and other information sources for Open University students on higher level courses in 1976', *Teaching at a distance*, **11**, 1978, 65−9.

Haworth, E. D., 'Library services to the off-campus and independent learner: a review of the literature', *Journal of librarianship,* **14**, (3), 1982, 157−75.

Henderson, W. (ed.), *Teaching academic subjects to adults: continuing education in practice*, University of Birmingham, Department of Extramural Studies, 1985.

Library Association of Australia, *Guidelines for library service to external students*, Ultimo (NSW), Library Association of Australia, 1982.

Marsterson, W. A. J. and Wilson, T. D., 'Home-based students and libraries', *Libri,* **25**, (3), 1975, 213−26.

Orton, L. and Wiseman, J., 'Library service to part-time students', *Canadian library journal*, **34**, (1), 1977, 23−7.

Parker, A. and Raybould, S. G. (eds.), *University studies for adults*, London, M. Joseph, 1972.

Smithers, A. and Griffin, A., *The progress of mature students*, Manchester, Joint Matriculation Board, 1986.

Tight, M., *Part-time degree level study in the United Kingdom*, Leicester, ACACE, 1982.

Titmus, C. (ed.), *Widening the field: continuing education in higher education*, Guildford, Society for Research into Higher Education, 1985.

Winter, A. and Cameron, M., *External students and their libraries*, Geelong (Victoria), Deakin University, 1983.

9 SUMMARY OF MAIN RECOMMENDATIONS, WITH CHECKLISTS FOR EVALUATING SERVICES

9.1 Scope and method

In this chapter the most important recommendations are repeated according to their original groupings, and with each recommendation a list of statements is given which is designed as an aid in judging the adequacy of that particular component of the library service. The statements cannot be completely comprehensive, objective, or mutually exclusive, but if carefully checked they should give some indication of the strengths and weaknesses in a library's services to adult continuing education. In its format the checklist is heavily indebted to two documents produced by the Association of College and Research Libraries.[1]

Each recommendation is followed by a continuum of four statements which relate to it. These statements represent the checklist. The evaluator should determine which of the four statements best describes the library concerned. To the left of each statement are three numbers, ranging from 1 to 12. If the statement chosen accurately describes the library, circle the middle number (2,5,8, or 11). If the evaluator feels the conditions of the library are below those described by the statement, circle the higher numbers (3,6,9, or 12). If the conditions of the library are above those of the statement, circle one of the lower numbers (1,4,7, or 10). Only one of the numbers in the 1−12 grouping should be circled. Finally, the marks from each item of the checklist should be transferred to the chart at the end of its section. The resulting graph should indicate those components in which the library is either strong or weak.

9.2 Group 1. General guidelines

A. The place of adult learners in library policy.
A library's policy statement should include the needs of adult learners (3.1).

1   2   3   The library has produced a policy statement, based on a community profile, in which due weight has been given to the needs of adult learners.

4   5   6   Although the library has produced a community profile, it has only an unwritten policy (which includes the needs of adult learners).

7   8   9   While the library's aims and objectives are unclear (no community survey has been carried out), the needs of adult learners seem not to have been overlooked.

10 11 12 The library has no clear policy, and as a result no attention has been paid specifically to the needs of adult learners.

B.   Staff responsibility

A member of the library staff should be given full responsibility for services to adult learners (3.2).

1   2   3   A senior member of the library staff has been assigned responsibility for services to adult learners and for the use of resources to that end.

4   5   6   A junior member of the library staff has been asked to co-ordinate services to adult learners (without a senior to be responsible to).

7   8   9   Library services to adult learners are carried out only when staff are available to do so.

10 11 12 No library services are carried out which are specifically aimed at adult learners.

C.   Institutional links

There should be close co-operation between the library and the relevant educational institutions (3.2.1).

1   2   3   The library works in close formal co-operation with relevant institutions such as the educational information and guidance service, voluntary societies, and other libraries.

4   5   6   There are some regular but informal links between the library and other relevant educational institutions.

7 8 9 The library has occasional contacts with other educational institutions.

10 11 12 The library has no links with any educational institutions.

D. Funding

Once a service to adult learners has been established, it should be regularly funded (3.2, 3.3).

1 2 3 Funds for services to adult learners are allocated as part of the annual library budget.

4 5 6 Funds for services to adult learners usually feature as part of the annual library budget.

7 8 9 Funds are occasionally allocated by the library for services to adult learners.

10 11 12 No funds are allocated for library services to adult learners.

E. Evaluation

Once a service to adult learners has been established it should be regularly monitored and evaluated in order to maintain its effectiveness (3.3).

1 2 3 Regular surveys are carried out, and statistics compiled, in order to monitor the effectiveness of the service to adult learners.

4 5 6 Occasional surveys are carried out in an attempt to evaluate the service to adult learners.

7 8 9 Enquiries are occasionally made about the working of the service to adult learners.

10 11 12 No attempt is made to evaluate the effectiveness of the service to adult learners.

Chart 1: General guidelines	Strong											Weak
The place of adult learners in library policy	1	2	3	4	5	6	7	8	9	10	11	12
Staff responsibility	1	2	3	4	5	6	7	8	9	10	11	12
Institutional links	1	2	3	4	5	6	7	8	9	10	11	12
Funding	1	2	3	4	5	6	7	8	9	10	11	12
Evaluation	1	2	3	4	5	6	7	8	9	10	11	12

9.3 Group 2. Public libraries and adult independent learners

A. Development plan
Each public library authority should produce a development plan for meeting the needs of independent learners (4.2.1).

1 2 3 The library authority has produced a detailed development plan for meeting the needs of independent learners.

4 5 6 The library authority has reviewed its services to independent learners and produced some brief guidance notes.

7 8 9 Some interest has been expressed in developing a service for independent learners, but no action has been taken.

10 11 12 The library authority does not recognize that independent learners have specific needs, and has therefore made no plans.

B. Staff training
Each public library authority should adopt programmes of training designed to help staff improve their assistance to adult learners (4.2.2).

1 2 3 The library authority has a comprehensive programme for training staff in assessing the needs of independent learners and in methods of improving services to them.

4 5 6 The library authority arranges occasional training sessions for staff in serving the needs of independent learners.

7 8 9 The library authority has occasional training sessions for staff, but few of them are specifically concerned with adult independent learning.

10 11 12 The library authority has no training programme for staff.

C. Access to materials

Each public library authority should provide access to a comprehensive range of self-instructional materials, open-learning packages, and audio-visual and broadcast materials and hardware (4.5.2—5).

1 2 3 The library authority's collection development policy includes the provision of a comprehensive range of materials specially designed for adult independent learners.

4 5 6 The library authority's collection development policy includes the selective acquisition of self-instructional and other materials designed for independent learners.

7 8 9 The library authority's collection development policy does not include the acquisition of materials specially designed for independent learners, but happens to have acquired a small selection.

10 11 12 The library authority does not recognize that independent learners need self-instructional materials and it does not acquire them.

D. Guidance and support services

Each public library authority should offer appropriate guidance and support services for independent learners, such as help with planning learning, help with selecting materials, training to use the library more effectively, and help with reading and study skills (4.6.1—4).

1 2 3 The library authority has a comprehensive programme of guidance and support services for independent learners, including the less traditional services of help with planning learning and help with reading and study skills.

4 5 6 The library authority has a programme of support services for independent learners, but it is confined to the traditional services of help with selecting materials and library instruction.

7 8 9 The library authority does not have a policy of support services for independent learners, but it does in practice provide some of the traditional services.

10 11 12 The library authority offers no support services specifically for independent learners.

E. Publicity

Each public library authority should publicize (to the general public) its own stock and its services to independent learners (4.5.1).

1 2 3 The library authority has an active policy of publicizing its stock as widely as possible and promoting its use, and of publicizing its services to independent learners.

4 5 6 The library authority produces publicity materials promoting the use of its stock but these are not widely distributed and they do not specifically mention services for independent learners.

7 8 9 The library authority produces printed guides to its stock and services, but these do not specifically mention services for independent learners, and they are made available only on library premises..

10 11 12 The library authority does not produce any publicity materials either for the general public or for any particular groups

---

Chart 2: Public libraries and adult independent learners

	Strong											Weak
Development plan	1	2	3	4	5	6	7	8	9	10	11	12
Staff training	1	2	3	4	5	6	7	8	9	10	11	12
Access to materials	1	2	3	4	5	6	7	8	9	10	11	12
Guidance and support services	1	2	3	4	5	6	7	8	9	10	11	12
Publicity	1	2	3	4	5	6	7	8	9	10	11	12

9.4 Group 3. Public libraries and adult students

A. Adult education publicity materials
Each public library should maintain and display the publicity materials of all local adult education providers (5.3).

1   2   3   All central and branch libraries regularly receive, and continuously display, all the publicity materials of the local adult education providers.

4   5   6   Some libraries receive publicity materials on a regular basis, but only a few make a point of displaying it continuously.

7   8   9   A few libraries receive publicity materials, but only irregularly, and none displays it continuously.

10 11 12 There are no arrangements for distributing publicity materials to public libraries, so that none of it is made available to the public through this channel.

B. Educational guidance
Each public library authority should participate in the work of the local Educational Guidance Unit (5.3).

1   2   3   The public library authority is a major component of the local Educational Guidance Unit, and public librarians play an active part in the Unit's operations.

4   5   6   The library authority is represented on the management committee of the local Unit, but none of the library staff is involved in the Unit's day-to-day operations.

7   8   9   The library authority has expressed an interest in the local Unit but plays no part in its operations.

10 11 12 The library authority has no involvement in the work of the local Unit.

C. User education
Each public library authority should arrange programmes of library instruction for local adult classes and individual students (5.5).

1 2 3 The public library authority actively encourages adult education tutors to take their students to the local library for instruction, and arranges programmes for individual home-based students.

4 5 6 The library authority arranges user education sessions for classes and individual students on request.

7 8 9 The library staff show members of the general public how to use the library when requested.

10 11 12 No library instruction is given to any library users.

D. Book supply for adult classes

Public libraries should provide book-boxes for adult education classes, where there is a special need (5.6).

1 2 3 The library authority's policy is to supply book-boxes to the meeting-place for any adult education classes (university, WEA or LEA) where there is a need.

4 5 6 The library's policy is to assemble special collections of books on library premises, for use by adult classes.

7 8 9 The library makes no special provision of materials for adult classes, but supplies adult tutors with sectional lists of holdings, where these are available.

10 11 12 The library has no arrangements for serving adult education classes.

E. Staff responsibility

Each public library should assign to a senior member of staff responsibility for services to adult education (5.7).

1 2 3 The library authority has a senior member of staff responsible for services to adult education, with a representative at each central and branch library.

4 5 6 The library authority has assigned responsibility for services to adult education to one member of the professional staff.

7 8 9 Library services to adult education are carried out only when staff are available to do so.

10 11 12 The library's policy does not include the concept of adult education as an activity requiring a service, and no staff are assigned to provide such a service.

F. Institutional links

Formal links should be maintained between the public library service and adult education bodies (5.7).

1 2 3 Public library staff and adult education practitioners meet on a regular basis through the medium of a local co-ordinating committee or similar body.

4 5 6 Public library and adult education staff meet occasionally *ad hoc* as need arises.

7 8 9 Public library and adult education staff have occasional contact by telephone or correspondence.

10 11 12 There is no communication between public library and adult education staff.

Chart 3: Public libraries and adult students

	Strong									Weak		
Adult education publicity materials	1	2	3	4	5	6	7	8	9	10	11	12
Educational guidance	1	2	3	4	5	6	7	8	9	10	11	12
User education	1	2	3	4	5	6	7	8	9	10	11	12
Book supply for adult classes	1	2	3	4	5	6	7	8	9	10	11	12
Staff responsibility	1	2	3	4	5	6	7	8	9	10	11	12
Institutional links	1	2	3	4	5	6	7	8	9	10	11	12

9.5 Group 4. College libraries and adult students

A. Access to library services

The college library and its services should be available not only to all registered college students but to the local community as a whole (6.3).

1 2 3 The college library's services and facilities are available on equal terms to all its registered students, all open learning students, and all members of the local community.

| 4 | 5 | 6 | Full library membership is available to all college (and other local) students registered on formal courses, and 'reference only' facilities for other members of the local community. |

4 5 6 Full library membership is available to all college (and other local) students registered on formal courses, and 'reference only' facilities for other members of the local community.

7 8 9 Full library membership is available only to registered college students (full-time and part-time), and 'reference only' facilities to other local students and residents.

10 11 12 Library membership is available only to college students on 'mainstream' courses; other students and local residents are not allowed access to the library.

B. Opening hours, study space and loans policy
Opening hours, study space and loans policy should all take account of the needs of part-time and short-course students (6.3.1, 6.3.2, 6.4.1, 6.4.2).

1 2 3 The library is open until late evening, has study space allowance for unattached learners, allows extended short-loan periods for part-time students, and provides class collections at out-centres.

4 5 6 The library is open until mid-evening, has adequate study space for all regular users, and allows extended short loan periods for a limited number of part-time students.

7 8 9 The library is open for a short period on some evenings, its study space is adequate for full-time students, but not for part-timers as well, and it makes no special loans provision for the latter.

10 11 12 The library is closed every evening, has inadequate space for full-time students, and does not allow loans to part-time students.

C. User education
Library instruction programmes should include adult students, and should take account of (and draw on) their special experience (6.5.1, 6.5.2).

1 2 3 The library provides information skills instruction to all full-time and part-time college students and tailors its programme to take account of the needs and experience of adults.

4 5 6 The library provides the same instruction programme for all college students, while recognizing the special needs of adults.

7 8 9 The library staff show students how to use the library when requested.

10 11 12 No library instruction is given to any library users.

D. Open learning students and independent learners

Library staff should give guidance and support to open learning students and independent learners (6.6.1.1, 6.6.1.2).

1 2 3 The library staff have a programme for giving regular study guidance to independent learners and regular assistance to open learning students in the use of materials.

4 5 6 The library staff give occasional study guidance to independent learners and occasional assistance to open learning students.

7 8 9 The library staff give some help, when asked, to independent learners and open learning students.

10 11 12 The library offers no support services specifically for independent learners or open learning students.

E. Staffing and funding

Library staffing and funding should be sufficient to support the additional materials and services implied in the above recommendations (6.8).

1 2 3 Funds for services to adult students are allocated as part of the annual library budget, and sufficient staff are employed to operate these services effectively.

4 5 6 Funds for services to adult students occasionally feature as part of the annual library budget, and

attempts are made to appoint staff with special responsibility for them.

7 8 9 There are no special funds for services to adult students, and staff try to fit these services into their existing responsibilities.

10 11 12 No funds are allocated for library services to adult students, and staff do not attempt to carry out any special services for them.

Chart 4: College libraries and adult students

	Strong											Weak
Access to library services	1	2	3	4	5	6	7	8	9	0	11	12
Opening hours, study space and loans policy	1	2	3	4	5	6	7	8	9	10	11	12
User education	1	2	3	4	5	6	7	8	9	10	11	12
Open learning students and independent learners	1	2	3	4	5	6	7	8	9	10	11	12
Staffing and funding	1	2	3	4	5	6	7	8	9	10	11	12

9.6 Group 5. Polytechnic libraries and adult students

A.   Assessing the needs of continuing education students

Libraries must develop ways of obtaining the views of non-traditional students on their needs for and use of library services, and should monitor usage of the library by specific groups of continuing education students (7.2.2.2−3).

1 2 3 The polytechnic library has fully investigated the library needs of continuing education students, monitored their usage of the library, and tailored services to meet their needs.

4 5 6 The library has obtained the views of continuing education students on their library needs, and investigated their usage of the library, but has made no subsequent changes to library policy.

7 8 9 The library has given some consideration to the library needs of continuing education students, but has not monitored their usage of the library and has made no changes to library policy.

91

10 11 12 The library has given no consideration to the library needs of continuing education students.

B. Staff collaboration and support

Library staff should work closely with the teaching and administrative staff who are concerned with continuing education courses, and should support polytechnic initiatives in continuing education (7.2.3.1–5).

1 2 3 Library staff work closely with teaching staff in the planning and development of continuing education courses and are actively associated with the polytechnic's initiatives in this field.

4 5 6 Library staff have some involvement in the planning of continuing education courses and in the polytechnic's initiatives in this field.

7 8 9 Library staff are aware of the developments in continuing education at the polytechnic but are not involved in them.

10 11 12 Library staff are unaware of, and have no involvement in, any of the developments in continuing education at the polytechnic.

C. Budget allocation

The additional costs of providing effective library services to non-traditional students should be recognized by the polytechnic and adequate funds should be allocated (7.2.5.1–3).

1 2 3 The library has transferred some resources away from traditional full-time students towards continuing education students and has convinced the polytechnic authorities that effective services to non-traditional students will incur additional costs.

4 5 6 The library has transferred some resources away from traditional full-time students towards continuing education students, but has failed to convey the message to the polytechnic that effective services to the latter will incur additional library costs.

7 8 9 The library allocates a very small proportion of its funds for services to continuing education students, and there is no prospect of any additional funds being made available.

10 11 12 The library allocates no funds for services to continuing education students.

D. Core collections and loan lengths

Libraries should consider creating special textbook collections for part-time students and variable loan lengths for different groups of students (7.2.4.6–7).

1 2 3 The library has established a core collection for the use solely of continuing education students and has introduced longer loan periods for part-time, distance and mature students.

4 5 6 The library has made some special purchases for continuing education students, largely for incorporation into the existing short-loan collection, but a separate collection for their use has not been established.

7 8 9 The library has considered the possibility of establishing a core collection, and of making special purchases, but has taken no action.

10 11 12 The library has given no consideration to the possibility of a core collection or of changing loan lengths.

E. User education

The acquisition of library skills should be regarded as a particular need of part-time students and should be incorporated into course design wherever appropriate (7.2.4.3).

1 2 3 It has been recognized that continuing education students may have particular problems in using the library effectively, and a comprehensive orientation programme has been introduced for them.

4 5 6 It has been recognized that continuing education students may have particular problems in using the

library, and arrangements have been made to include them in the existing orientation programme.

7   8   9 The library has an orientation programme, but the particular problems of continuing education students have not been recognized.

10 11 12 The library has no user education programme.

Chart 5: Polytechnic libraries and adult students

	Strong											Weak
Assessing the needs of continuing												
education students	1	2	3	4	5	6	7	8	9	10	11	12
Staff collaboration and support	1	2	3	4	5	6	7	8	9	10	11	12
Budget allocation	1	2	3	4	5	6	7	8	9	10	11	12
Core collection and loan lengths	1	2	3	4	5	6	7	8	9	10	11	12
User education	1	2	3	4	5	6	7	8	9	10	11	12

9.7   Group 6. University libraries and adult students

A.   Budget allocation

A university should provide regular financial support for the library services to its continuing education courses (8.3.1, 8.3.2).

1   2   3 Funds for library services to the entire programme of continuing education courses are allocated as part of the annual library budget.

4   5   6 Funds for library services to some continuing education courses are allocated on a regular basis.

7   8   9 Funds are used for library services to continuing education courses only occasionally.

10 11 12 No funds are provided for library services to continuing education courses.

B.   Staff

At each appropriate on-campus library a professional librarian should be assigned responsibility for services to continuing education courses (8.3.1, 8.3.3).

94

1 2 3 Professional library staff (at central and departmental libraries) are given the specific responsibility for providing library services to continuing education courses.

4 5 6 Library services to continuing education courses are provided regularly by whatever library staff are available.

7 8 9 Library services to continuing education courses are provided only occasionally by whatever library staff are available.

10 11 12 No library staff have responsibility for services to continuing education courses, and such services are rarely or never provided.

C. Special services

A university library should make special arrangements for its adult students in relation to opening hours, user education and access to catalogues (8.3.5).

1 2 3 A special programme for adult students has been implemented, including longer opening hours, library instruction at times convenient to them, and off-campus access to catalogues.

4 5 6 Some attempt has been made at implementing a special programme for adult students, but only a proportion of the measures have been carried out.

7 8 9 Only one innovation has been made in respect of services to adult students.

10 11 12 No special arrangements for adult students have been made.

D. Core collections

Core collections, reserved for the use of continuing education students, should be built up (8.3.4).

1 2 3 Core collections have been established largely as an alternative to short-loan collections and reserved

solely for the use of part-time adult and continuing education students on campus.

4 5 6 Some special purchases have been made for part-time and continuing education students but these have been incorporated into the existing short-loan collection.

7 8 9 Adult students are entitled to use the short-loan collection, but no special purchases have been made for them.

10 11 12 Adult students are not entitled to use the short-loan collection.

E.   Extramural courses

Extramural courses should normally be served by a separate extramural library, concentrating on the supply of special collections to off-campus locations (8.4.1).

1 2 3 The university's department of extramural studies (or its equivalent) has its own regularly and adequately funded library, whose sole purpose is to serve the needs of extramural students and tutors.

4 5 6 The department of extramural studies has its own library, but it is inadequately funded and many extramural courses have to rely on the services of other (university and public) libraries.

7 8 9 The department of extramural studies has no library of its own and all its courses have to rely on the services of other libraries.

10 11 12 The university's programme of extramural courses receives no services from any libraries.

Chart 6: University libraries and adult students

	Strong											Weak
Budget allocation	1	2	3	4	5	6	7	8	9	10	11	12
Staff	1	2	3	4	5	6	7	8	9	10	11	12
Special services	1	2	3	4	5	6	7	8	9	10	11	12
Core collections	1	2	3	4	5	6	7	8	9	10	11	12
Extramural courses	1	2	3	4	5	6	7	8	9	10	11	12

Reference

1 Association of College and Research Libraries, 'An evaluative checklist for reviewing library services to extension/non-campus students', *College and research libraries news*, **41**, (9), 1980, 268–72, which is in turn based on *An evaluative checklist for reviewing a college library program* developed by ACRL.

CUMULATIVE BIBLIOGRAPHY

All the items previously listed are included here, together with some additions.

Adult education and public libraries in the 1980s: a symposium, London, The Library Association, 1980.

Advisory Council for Adult and Continuing Education, *Distance learning and adult students: a review of recent developments in the public education sector*, Leicester, ACACE, 1983.

Advisory Council for Adult and Continuing Education, *Links to learning: a report on educational information, advisory and counselling services for adults*, Leicester, ACACE, 1979.

Advisory Council for Adult and Continuing Education, *A strategy for the basic education of adults*, Leicester, ACACE, 1979.

Allred, J., *The measurement of library services: an appraisal of current problems and possibilities*, Bradford, MCB Publications, 1979.

Allred, J. and Hay, W., *A preliminary study of the involvement of public libraries with adult learners: final report*, Leeds, Leeds Polytechnic School of Librarianship, 1979.

Anderson, J. and Boyle, J., *Public libraries and educational broadcasting*, Penzance, Public Libraries Group of the Library Association, 1980.

Association of College and Research Libraries, 'Guidelines for extended campus library services', *College and research libraries news*, **43**, (3), 1982, 86−8.

Association of College and Research Libraries, 'Standards of college libraries, 1985', *College and research libraries news,* **46**, (5), 1985, 241−52.

Bailey, R. H., 'What's all this about university standards?', *Adult education*, **59**, (3), 1986, 227−32.

Baker, D. (ed.), *Student reading needs and higher education*, London, Library Association Publishing Ltd, 1986.

Bevan, N., 'Library services and the part-time student', in Fletcher, J. (ed.), *Reader services in polytechnic libraries*, Aldershot, Gower in association with COPOL, 1985, 159−83.

Birge, L. E., *Serving adult learners: a public library tradition*, Chicago, American Library Association, 1981.

Blagden, P., *The library needs of part-time students preparing for professional examinations*, (Library Research Digest No. 10), London, City of London Polytechnic, LRRS Publications, 1984.

Brockman, J. R. and Klobas, J. E., *Libraries and books in distance education*, Perth, Western Australia Institute of Technology, 1983.

Brookfield, S. D., 'The adult learning iceberg: a critical review of the work of Allen Tough', *Adult education*, **54**, 1981, 110−18.

Brookfield, S., 'Independent adult learning', *Studies in adult education*, **13**, (1), 1981, 15−27.

Butler, L., *Educational guidance for adults: some terms, definitions and issues in the practice of educational guidance by independent services and public libraries*, Leicester, ACACE, 1982.

Butler, L., *Information and technology in educational guidance for adults*, Leicester, UDSACE, 1986.

Coleman, P. M., *Whose problem? the public library and the disadvantaged*, London, Association of Assistant Librarians, 1981.

Council for Educational Technology, *Learning resources in colleges: their organization and management*, London, CET, 1981.

Craig, R. and Gerver, E. (eds.), *Lights in the darkness: Scottish libraries and adult education*, Edinburgh, Scottish Institute of Adult Education, 1985.

Dale, S., *Guidelines for training in libraries, 8. Distance learning*, London, Library Association, 1986.

Dale, S., 'Another way forward for adult learners: the public library and independent study', *Studies in adult education*, **12**, (1), 1980, 29−38.

Dale, S. and Carty, J., *Finding out about continuing education:*

sources of information and their use, Milton Keynes, Open University Press, 1985.

Davidson, D. E., 'What will be the bandwagon of the 1980s?', *U C & R newsletter*, **1**, 1980, 7.

Davies, D. and Robertson, D., 'Open college: towards a new view of adult education', *Adult education*, **59**, (2), 1986, 106–114.

Davies, J. H., 'Adults and reading', in Thornton, A. H. and Stephens, M. D. (eds.), *The university in its region*, University of Nottingham, Department of Adult Education, 1977, 100–9.

Department of Education and Science, *Adult education: a plan for development*, (Russell Report), London, HMSO, 1973.

Department of Education and Science, *The development of higher education into the 1990s*, (Cmnd. 9524), London, HMSO, 1985. (See esp. Chapter 4 'Education throughout life'.)

Department of Education and Science, *Public libraries and cultural activities*, London, HMSO, 1975.

Drodge, S., *Adult education library provision*, Leicester, East Midlands Branch of the Library Association, 1984.

Drodge, S., 'Libraries and adult learners: future developments', *Journal of librarianship*, **16**, (3), 1984, 170–87.

Fisher, R. K., *The libraries of university departments of adult education and extramural studies*, (LA pamphlet 36), London, Library Association, 1974.

Fisher, R. K., 'Library services for university adult education: a neglected area', *Adult education*, **53**, (6), 1981, 372–5.

Fisher, R. K., *Library services to university extension students in the USA*, London, British Library Research and Development Department (report no. 5432), 1978.

Fisher, R. K., 'Regional libraries for adult education', *Journal of librarianship*, **3**, (4), 1971, 228–36.

Further Education Unit, *The experience of open learning: a summary document*, London, FEU, 1985.

Gains, D., 'Libraries and other information sources for Open University students on higher level courses in 1976', *Teaching at a distance*, **11**, 1978, 65–9.

Haworth, E. D., 'Library services to the off-campus and independent learner: a review of the literature', *Journal of librarianship*, **14**, (3), 1982, 157–75.

Heeks, P., *Library adult education: the unfilled promise*, Winchester, Public Libraries Research Group, 1982.

Henderson, W. (ed.), *Teaching academic subjects to adults: continuing education in practice*, Birmingham, University of Birmingham, Department of Extramural Studies, 1985.

Hoggart, R. and others, *Continuing education within universities and polytechnics*, Leicester, ACACE, 1983.

Jennings, B., *The education of adults in Britain: a study of organization, finance and policy*, Hull, University of Hull Department of Adult and Continuing Education, 1985.

Kennedy, D., *How do I cope? teaching and support in continuing education*, Sheffield, Association for Recurrent Education, 1983.

Latcham, J. and Kelly, L. U., *Open learning: an introductory reading list*, Coombe Lodge, The Further Education Staff College, 1986.

Lessin, B. M. (ed.), *The Off-Campus library Services Conference proceedings: I, St Louis, Missouri, October 14–15, 1982*, Mt Pleasant (Michigan), Central Michigan University Press, 1983.

Lewis, D., 'Continuing education', *Library Association record*, **82**, (4), 1980, 175.

Lewis, D., 'LA and continuing education', *Library Association record*, **83**, (9), 1981, 409–10.

The Library Association, *College libraries: guidelines for professional service and resource provision*, London, Library Association, 3rd edn, 1982.

The Library Association, *Standards for university extra-mural libraries*, London, The Library Association, 1978.

The Library Association, London and Home Counties Branch, *Libraries and open learning*, Orpington, Library Association London and Home Counties Branch, 1985.

The Library Association, University College and Research Section, *Open learning and its impact on academic libraries*, Nottingham, LA UC & R Section, 1985.

The Library Association of Australia, *Guidelines for library serv-*

ices to external students, ed. C. Crocker, Ultimo (NSW), Library Association of Australia, 1982.

Lubans, J. (ed.), *Educating the public library user*, Chicago, American Library Association, 1983.

Lucas, S. and Ward, P. (eds.), *A survey of 'access' courses in England*, Lancaster, University of Lancaster School of Education, 1985.

McDowell, E., *Part-time students and libraries: the results of research studies at Newcastle upon Tyne Polytechnic Library*, Newcastle upon Tyne Polytechnic Products Ltd, 1985.

Marsterson, W. A. J. and Wilson, T. D., 'Home based students and libraries', *Libri*, **25**, (3), 1975, 213–26.

Monaco, J., 'Public libraries and adult independent learners: an action research programme', *Journal of community education*, **4**, (1), 1985, 14–20.

National Institute of Adult Continuing Education, *Yearbook of adult continuing education 1986–87*, Leicester, NIACE, 1986.

Neale, B., *An investigation of the learning needs of adults in Islington*, London, Inner London Education Authority/London Borough of Islington, Library Service, 1983.

Newman, M., *The poor cousin: a study of adult education*, London, Allen & Unwin, 1979.

Open Learning Federation, *Newsletter* (3 a year), Barnet, Barnet College.

Open University, *Adults and education (Unit 14 of Course E222, The control of education in Britain)*, Milton Keynes, Open University Press, 1979.

Orton, L. and Wiseman, J., 'Library services to part-time students', *Canadian library journal*, **34**, (1), 1977, 23–7.

Parker, A. and Raybould, S. G. (eds.), *University studies for adults*, London, M. Joseph, 1972.

Pates, A. and others (eds.), *Second chance 1984–85: the annual guide to adult education and training opportunities*, Milton Keynes, National Extension College, 1984.

Payne, P. (ed.), *The part-time student in the library: papers prepared for a conference held at City of London Polytechnic April 15th and 16th 1982*, London, LLRS Publications, 1983.

Percy, K. and Ramsden, P., *Independent study: two examples from English higher education*, Guildford, Society for Research into Higher Education, 1980.

Percy, K. A. and Willett, I. H. (eds.), *Libraries and the future of adult education*, Lancaster, University of Lancaster, 1981.

Pritchard, A. and Payne, P., *Part-time students: their use of a polytechnic library*, London, LLRS Publications, 1980.

Public Libraries and Adult Education Committee for the North-West, *Guidelines for co-operation*, Liverpool: WEA West Lancashire and Cheshire District, 1978.

Publishers Association, *Booktrade yearbook 1986*, London, Publishers Association, 1986.

Smith, V., *Public libraries and adult independent learners: a report* (CET working papers, 27), London, Council for Educational Technology, 1987.

Smithers, A. and Griffin, A., *The progress of mature students*, Manchester, Joint Matriculation Board, 1986.

Stock, A., *Adult education in Great Britain*, Leicester, NIACE, 1978.

Surridge, R. and Bowen, J., *The Independent Learning Project: a study of changing attitudes in American public libraries*, Brighton, Public Libraries Research Group, 1977.

Tight, M., *Part-time degrees, diplomas and certificates: a guide to part-time higher education courses at universities, polytechnics and colleges*, Cambridge, Hobsons, 1986.

Tight, M., *Part-time degree level study in the United Kingdom*, Leicester, ACACE, 1982.

Titmus, C. (ed.), *Widening the field: continuing education in higher education*, Guildford, Society for Research into Higher Education, 1985.

Tough, A., *The adult's learning projects*, Toronto, Ontario Institute for Studies in Education, 1971.

Turner, N., 'Libraries and community education', *Scottish journal of adult education*, **6**, (2), 1983, 23–7.

Unit for the Development of Adult Continuing Education, *The challenge of change: developing educational guidance for adults*, Leicester, National Institute of Adult Continuing Education, 1986.

University Grants Committee, *Report of the Continuing Education Working Party*, London, UGC, 1984.

Urquhart, D. J. and Irving, A., *Access to libraries: a study of methodology*, Loughborough, Loughborough University Department of Library and Information Studies, 1978.

Ward, M. L., *Readers and library users: a study of reading habits and public library use*, London, Library Association, 1978.

Wilson, T. D. and Marsterson, W. A. J., *Local library co-operation: final report on a project funded by the Department of Education and Science*, Sheffield, University of Sheffield Postgraduate School of Librarianship and Information Science, 1974.

Winter, A. and Cameron, M., *External students and their libraries*, Geelong, Australia, Deakin University, 1983.

INDEX

References are to section numbers (except for the single numbers, which refer to whole chapters).

Public libraries
  and adult students, 5, 9.4
  and independent learning, 4,
    9.3
Public Libraries and Adult
    Independent Learning
    Project, 1.2.1, 4

Reading, record of, 2.1.6, 4.6.6
Reading skills, 2.1.6, 2.2.15,
    4.6.4, 9.3(D)
Regional Library Systems, 5.7
Regional libraries for adult
    education, 3.2.1
Research projects, 5.7(d)
Residential colleges, 2.2.7

Self-help service, 4.2.2, 4.6.2
Self-instructional materials,
    2.1.4, 4.7(j), 4.9, 9.3(C)
Short-loan collections
  college libraries, 6.4.1, 9.5(B)
  polytechnic libraries, 7.2.4.7,
    9.6(D)
  university libraries, 8.3.4,
    8.4.3, 9.7(D)
Societies (local), 2.1.4, 4.2
Special libraries, 3.1.1
Staff training, 4.6.1, 4.7(c), 5.4,
    5.7, 7.2.6.1, 9.3(B)
Staffing, 3.2, 4.2.1, 4.7(b),
    5.2(d), 5.8(f), 6.8, 8.3.3,
    8.5(b), 9.2(B), 9.4(E),
    9.5(E), 9.7(B)
Standards, 1.3.1

*Standards for university extra-
    mural libraries*, 1.2.1, 8.4.1
Study skills, 2.1.6, 2.2.15, 4.6.4,
    5.5, 6.5, 7.2.4.3, 9.3(D)
Study space, 2.1.5, 2.2.17
  college libraries, 6.3.1, 9.5(B)
  public libraries, 4.5.6, 5.6(j)
Subject specialists, access to,
    4.6.5

Telephone service, 7.2.4.4
Training Access Points (TAP),
    4.4.7, 5.3

Unemployed persons, 2.1.2,
    4.4.6
Unit for the Development of
    Adult Continuing Education
    (UDACE), 5.4
Universities, 2.2.9, 8, 9.7
User education, 2.1.6, 2.2.15,
    2.2.17
  college libraries, 6.5, 9.5(B)
  polytechnic libraries, 7.2.4.3,
    7.2.7(e), 9.6(E)
  university libraries, 8.3.5(c),
    8.5(d), 9.7(C)
  public libraries, 4.6.3, 5.5,
    5.8(c), 9.4(C)

Video materials, 4.4.3, 5.6(e),
    7.2.3.5

Workers Educational Association
    (WEA), 2.2.8, 5.6(c)

108